I NEED ANSWERS

I NEED ANSWERS

VOLUME ONE

How Important Is It For A Boy To
Have A Positive Male Role Model?

WRITTEN BY:
REZSAUN V. LEWIS

ILLUSTRATIONS BY:
CEDRIC TOLIVER II

EDITED BY:
SUE MILLER

Charleston, SC
www.PalmettoPublishing.com

I Need Answers, Volume One

First Edition

ISBN: 978-1-63837-052-9

THIS BOOK IS DEDICATED TO MY FATHER,
HERBERT LEE JENKINS JR.

TABLE OF CONTENTS

Purpose	ix
My Story	1
Dustin Rhodes	7
Mike Wilson	13
Byron Ray	18
Dennis Green	22
Herbert Jenkins Jr.	28
Cordarro Brown	31
"Johnny Phillips"	35
Stephan Whaley	40
Vincenio Dawkins Sr.	46
Omar Muhammad	54
Chris Bean	58
Kevin Rasberry	65
Thomas Chisolm	69
"Shawn Broughton"	73
Dante Pelzer	79
Jason Ellis	83
Jerome Colden	90
"Christopher Robinson"	95
McKendrick Dunn	98
Parting thoughts	103

PURPOSE

"All knowledge starts with a question" - ReZsaun Lewis.

Today is November 30th, 2017, and I'm sitting at my computer listening to Stevie Wonder's "If It's Magic," and I am contemplating what I am about to endeavor. There is so much to be done to complete this project. I've never written a book before, and I have no idea where to begin. I guess the best place to start is with the question, "Why would I write a book?"

Different people write for various reasons. Some write to share their life stories, like creating new and exciting worlds, and some to retell the stories of others who have done great things and overcome great odds.

My purpose for writing this book is to find answers to questions that have eaten at my very existence for a long time. I'm writing this book for those who have questions and just need that extra push to begin their journey to getting the answers they seek. However long it takes me to write this book, I'm trusting that God will guide my path and allow this to bless the life of someone who reads or listens to this book.

This book will be filled with questions I've asked myself and others over time. The answers are based on my research and spoken in an understandable language to any willing reader. I have no plans of this book being the average in any regard. My approach to this book is to seek knowledge and a sharer of the information I have pursued. My prayer is that someone is enlightened and learns something new that they may not have known or considered. I also endeavor to start discussions that will facilitate the healing needed for the divide that has consumed our country and world in recent times.

These short stories are based on my life experiences related to the questions I asked each person I interviewed. By reading or listening to this book, I hope you feel an attachment to me as the author and as a man. Though I don't know what will happen next, I know that this book's creation is a labor of love that will change my life forever. Thank you for taking this journey with me.

"We're here for a reason.
I believe a bit of the
reason is to throw little
torches out to lead people
through the dark."

– Whoopi Goldberg

MY STORY

Hometown: North Charleston, SC
Education Level: Associate Degree in Arts, Bachelor's Degree in Science (Elementary Education, Currently working on Master's Degree in Public Administration
Occupation: Executive Director, Lowcountry Youth Services
Married: Yes (13 years), 1 Divorce (4 years)
Kids: 5 (4 girls, 1 boy) (20, 18, 17, 13, 13)

Fatherly Presence

I had a great relationship with my father while growing up, even though he did not live in my home. I fondly remember visiting him as a child and how much I loved spending time with him. After he and my mom split, he had a daughter and ultimately married my stepmother. They went on to have another three children. Despite all of this, my father and I still had an extraordinary relationship.

Healthy Fear?

I, like many children growing up, had a healthy fear of my father. I can remember at a young age being terrified of my father in many ways. I remember when his disciplinary techniques would sometimes cross the line into actual child abuse. My father was arrested for one particular beating that went too far. This incident occurred in the middle of the street in my grandma's neighborhood. Maybe one day I'll write about it. After that incident, my father never hit me again. I was around 8-years-old at the time, but I still remember that day and what happened. Though that was the last time he ever put his hands on me, I knew he could act out again. That fear remained throughout our relationship, but the positive aspects of our relationship were never hurt by it.

Fondest Memories of Father

My fondest memories of my father growing up had a lot to do with visiting him and his family (my stepmother, brothers, and sisters) on the weekends and during the summer. There always seemed to be something going on, and they seemed to have so much fun. I also remember going to his softball games and watching him play. I thought my dad was the best softball player on the planet, and you couldn't tell me anything else.

My best memories of my dad are from when I became a man and a father myself. I could always find my dad, even if we went months without talking. I would go to his job; he'd clock out and speak to me until his break was over. We had a rule, "No news is good news." We meant that it wasn't necessary to call all the time to keep in touch. However, if the phone rings or one of us shows up, we would drop everything to talk. This worked well for us. Sometimes we'd meet to hang out and talk. Most of those times would take place at a local pool hall.

My dad loved playing pool, and I loved playing with him. I wanted to beat him so badly! Sometimes I did when I got better, but most of the time, he'd kick my butt. I can remember talking to my dad about everything during those talks, and there wasn't anything I couldn't tell him. He kept it pretty real with me because my dad was always a straight shooter.

Impact On Me as a Father

There are many ways that the history with my father impacts the way that I parent my children. First of all, growing up with my father not being in my home, made it crucial that my children are raised with me present. It is also essential that if they are not in my house, I will spend as much time with them as possible. This was one of the reasons why my divorce hurt me so much. I felt like I wouldn't have them with me as much as I wanted to and that I had failed them as a father. I remain determined to be there for my children and be a consistent force in their lives. That has worked in my favor though it hasn't always been easy.

Another way that my father's example impacts my parenting is that my dad would tell me that he loved me every time he saw me. I know it was important to him that I knew that. Saying 'I love you" is something that my children often hear thanks to the example set by my father. My father wasn't able to attend as many of my events (concerts, games, life achievements, etc.) as I would've liked as a child. I make it a priority to be present at every single event that I possibly can be at for my kids. I don't always make the mark, my kids remind me every time I miss anything, but I try my best to be there and have a pretty high percentage rate.

My father's disciplinary techniques have impacted the way I raise and discipline my children. I am not a big proponent of corporal punishment, but I have used it with my children from time to time. The times that I've made use of it, I'd like to think that it was warranted and wouldn't be considered "abuse," As I have grown as a man and a father, I use it less and less. I want my children to learn from their mistakes and that their mistakes have consequences. I don't want those consequences to be tied to a fear of me.

The final way I'm impacted by my father's example is the talks we used to have. I have made a life out of talking to my children about everything that they're feeling and going through. That's a direct result of what my dad and I would do. I try to take that to the next level by sometimes "forcing" a conversation even when my children aren't ready to talk to me. My dad had a way of making you feel like you could tell him anything, and he'd listen without judgment. I try to provide the same openness for my children.

Other Positive Males

I was blessed to have several men in my life who have stood in the gap for me and are at least in part responsible for the man that I am today. I have many uncles who have always been active in my life. The biggest inspiration and example of what a man should be was my grandfather, Joseph Capers.

In my eyes, my granddad had to be the coolest person ever to live. He was handsome, smooth, and hardworking. Man, did he LOVE ME! I learned so many things about manhood from my grandfather. Many of the things that I learned came as lessons without words.

When I was in the first grade, I lived with my grandparents because my mother worried about my school performance. This meant that I went from being one of three boys in a house with my mom to the only child in the house with my grandparents. My grandma, granddad, and I became thick as thieves during that period. My granddad and I were together every day.

In 3rd grade, I moved back in with my mother, and I would reflect on the times we would ride in his car listening to old-school music. I still have a great love for the '50s, 60's, 70's music to this day because of those rides. He did so many things for me.

When I joined the middle school chorus in the sixth grade, he would pick me up from home and take me to my rehearsals on weekends to miss one. He also washed my clothes for me and brought them to me to ensure that I would have stuff to wear for school. He bought me my first car, and he showed me how to take care of it. He taught me how a man should dress and take care of his hygiene.

My grandfather was the person that had the most significant impact on my life. He passed away in 2012 after a bout with cancer. I wasn't ready to let him go, and I still haven't completely gotten over his passing. There have been so many things that have transpired in my life that I would've loved for him to see and to be a part of. In everything I do, I always say to myself, "I wish granddad were here to see this." I miss him every day.

Mentorship

In my life, I've had the honor of serving youth in many capacities. In addition to being a father to my five beautiful children, I've been a youth sports coach, a teacher, and a mentor. For the past four years, I've served with Lowcountry Youth Services in many leadership positions and most recently became the Executive Director of this nonprofit organization.

With Lowcountry Youth Services, we endeavor to help young men from eight to eighteen years old become well-rounded men. Men who any college, corporation, or community would be proud to call their own. Men who raise their children love their wives and can express themselves effectively. That work is done in many ways that involve mentorship, learning leadership skills, and the cultivation of soft skills and life skills. Through my work with Lowcountry Youth Services, I've had the opportunity to build relationships with many young men and their families. I've been able to use my life experiences to help them better themselves. Most of all, I've been able to pass on the lessons that I've learned from the men that nurtured me.

Final Words for Father

My father passed away in 2018, and his passing hurt me a great deal. Cancer also took him away from me. The one good thing that came out of him having cancer was spending a lot of time together before he passed away. We talked a lot, and I was even able to interview him for this book. I can honestly say that when he died, there were no words that were left unsaid.

If I could say anything to him, I would tell him, "Thank you." I would thank him for being the father I needed to become the person and father I am today. I would thank him for always encouraging me to be my best self and for teaching me to take time to enjoy life because it is short. I'd thank him for the long talks and the short talks. Most of all, I'd thank him for being there and not abandoning me.

DUSTIN RHODES

Hometown: Summerville, SC
Education Level: Bachelor's degree in History and Secondary Education
Occupation: Middle School Teacher
Married: No
Kids: No

Dustin's father was in his life during his childhood. He speaks of how his father would take out his work frustrations on him and his mom. In particular, there was an incident when he was 16 years old where they were watching his favorite TV show, 'Family Matters.' His father walked in, shut the TV off, and told him to "get those 'n-words' off my TV." Although he grew up in a blue-collar neighborhood, Dustin hung around with only persons of color and had a black best friend. Although his father was present during his childhood, he was greatly affected by his father's perception of racism and his father's dry-drunk spells that affect how he views the world today.

His Father

Growing up, he was terrified of his father, especially when doing chores, as he would insult him if he missed out on doing things correctly. Being a military man for 22 years, his father learned how to project his voice and to use it to drive fear into him.

Dustin remembers only two occasions when his father put his hands on him, and he spoke about being whipped with a belt around 8 or 9 years old. He tells the story of an incident during his teen years when he was about 15 years old. He was playing basketball at a neighbor's house, and he was wearing baggy pants. This caused his boxers to show (he does admit to sagging his pants a little as it was a phase he went through growing up.) His father publicly yelled at him and, once inside their home, said to him, "You're not going to be there sagging your pants like an 'n-word'" and shoved him. His mother had to intervene as Dustin was about to push back in his defense.

He did not have a great relationship with his father while growing up. Dustin speaks of joining the military to make his father proud. His military career did not go so well, and he was discharged for minor disciplinary infractions. He did, however, receive an honorable discharge.

Dustin speaks of the changes he experienced in his father as he grew older. His father was a great supporter of Barack Obama and accused the Republican Party of only challenging Barack Obama because he was black. He shared another example of this change when his father openly hugged his best friend of color after being released from prison.

Although Dustin went on to have an improved relationship with his father during his older years, he still held a lot of resentment because of how his father treated him and his mother when he was growing up. Dustin felt that his father took a lot of his childhood away from him as a result. He still does not know what led to the significant change, but his mom believes it resulted from him moving away from the neighborhood they once lived in and into the country.

Dustin has learned that treating someone based on the color of their skin is illogical as you can only judge a person by the content of their character. He provides an example using his father. If he were to judge his father based on his skin color (his father was a southern white guy), he was just an old southern white guy. But if he were to judge him based on the content of his character, he would not be the most attractive of people. This conclusion had nothing to do with the color of his skin but with his attitude. This is why he can never judge the character of "colored people" until he first gets to know them.

Dustin described skin color as only a pigment tied to actions that are not scientifically rooted in biology but only in the social construction of what society views and what society makes up.

Dustin also shares that his father had a 'no excuse policy.' His father believed that every opportunity is for everybody regardless of one's situation or environment. The only difference is that there may be more doors than others for certain people to get that opportunity. Dustin believes that about 95% of people won't seize their opportunities because it is "too hard" or they find it easier to blame everyone else around them (i.e., politicians). It is up to each person to look into themselves and what they are doing to get better.

He shares a lesson his father once taught him. 'You can go to a rough school and live in a rough neighborhood where there is nothing but crime, drugs, and poverty, but there is a library somewhere. Dustin learned that rather than sit and blame the school system and everything else for the lack of being educated, people should go to a library and pick up a book, as education is self-liberating.

He had to learn the world by himself as his father was not around to teach him anything about how the world operated. He doesn't feel like his father was not there to guide him and teach him how to be a man. Dustin believes that he would have learned things a lot sooner if his father was in his life. He also believes that there is a divine reason for some fathers not being in their children's lives. Although some will think it a selfish act, it may be that their father just wasn't supposed to be there. Having him around could have possibly made their lives a lot worse.

Other Role Models

Dustin had a female role model in his life instead of a male role model. She was his karate instructor. He does not feel there was any significant impact on his life having a female role model. He states that many people believe that there are certain things that only a man can teach that a woman can't. He has yet to understand why he was introduced to fighting by a woman who held an eighth-degree black belt. He also shared the example of Tupac, whose father was not present when growing up, and he was taught everything by his mother and grew up to be a great man. Dustin believes that mothers should teach their children what they can. He, unfortunately, does not see this happening with many parents within this generation.

Making Daddy Proud

Dustin shared a memory of a sparring tournament he was in where he was awarded a gold medal and went from State to Regionals and then Nationals. He mentioned how proud his father was of him, especially after an incident in which he was unfairly scored. Dustin took it upon himself to hit his opponent during the sparring match. He believed all points were going towards him in what seemed to be a rigged match.

He shares that his father had a proud look on his face when he decided to stand up for himself.

He felt good as he finally felt that he was doing something well. Growing up, he felt like he was always messing up and couldn't do anything right when it came to his father. He finally felt like he was worth something and doing something that made his father proud.

Reflection

He thinks that many times people find excuses and blame the things they do on their father's absence, but that there must have been a point in their childhood when they realized that he was gone and was not coming back. This is where he believes educators and single mothers need to step in to teach that the decisions being made lies strictly on the shoulders of the individual. Dustin believes that these lessons have made him into the man he is today and does not regret growing up the way he did.

Dustin believes that life is all about perspective and what one makes of it. No one is going to have the same journey, mindset, or thoughts. Everybody's experience will be different because it is based on how our minds can control the narrative in how we see the world. He shared a few examples. "If you put five different people in the same environment/room, it is guaranteed that each of those five individuals is going to have a different experience." "If you put five different people in a deep freezer, they are all going to say it is cold, but when you ask them to describe certain things, everyone is going to describe something different."

Being a Role Model

Dustin believes he is a good role model for several reasons and admits to having anger issues that he had to learn to control during his late 20's. His desire to become a role model was based on the need he saw for those kids who lacked a role model in their lives. This was one of the main reasons why he decided to become a teacher.

He believes that he is a great role model in his perception of the world, philosophy, and no excuse policy. He instills this same policy in his students, who he states can have no excuse for not getting things done as it all comes down to managing their time.

Dustin shares experiences with others to let them know that he has been where they are. He has been broke, lived out of his car, done drugs, had days when he would blackout from being drunk, associated with gang members, played chauffeur to prostitutes as a means to earn money to feed himself, and all during his 20's. He does this to let them know that there is always an option, and it is up to them to decide if they are willing to do what it takes to be better.

He shares a story about a male patient he took care of in a short-term care facility where he worked. The patient was a high school drop-out and wanted to go back to school to obtain his GED to become a botanist. Dustin took it upon himself to research where the patient could enroll to get his GED and also where he could enroll in a Botany Program. He then took all this information to the patient as the first step to his 'other option'. He believes that although he can guide people and get them all the information they need, it is ultimately up to them to make the best choice.

Words for Dad

During this interview, Dustin shared that his father had passed away about three years ago. Dustin would like to tell him that he loved him and thank him for being the best person he knew he could be. He wishes he could still speak with him because he still has questions for him, and there is a lot he would like to know. Dustin regrets not discussing his childhood before his death and would ask him about his views on racism and if he was sorry for his perception back then. He would want his father to explain the effects of racism on society and how he used his bias as a fundamental life trait that he believes would have made things a lot easier than figuring it out independently, which was a lot harder.

MIKE WILSON

Hometown: Baltimore, MD
Education Level: 2 Associate Degrees, Bachelor's Degree
Occupation: Air Force, Aviation Resource Management
Married: Yes (2 1/2 years), 2 Divorces (4 years, 6 1/2 years)
Kids: 4 (2 girls, 2 boys) (14, 9, 2, 1 on the way)

Mike's father was not in his life growing up. He found out who his father was via an ancestry.com search the prior year to this interview. There was a man in his life as a "father figure"; however, he never took ownership of him and ended up putting him out of the house at 16 years old. He believed that Mike was his child; however, that proved not to be true. His style of parenting was such that he thought that by being around, he was a father. He didn't engage himself in the developmental aspects of parenthood necessary in the upbringing of a child. Mike believes that he's been intentional in not turning out like the man who "raised" him.

Are You My Dad?

The man who raised him was listed on his birth certificate as his father. He never took a DNA test but instead assumed that he was Mike's father after another man took a DNA test, and it came back as unfavorable. Though he claimed Mike as his son, he never actually took responsibility for his three other children, who biologically were his. He went out of his way to NOT be in his children's lives, believing that his children were only calling him for money. For this and many other reasons, Mike consciously decided he didn't want to be like his "father." He found out that this man was not his father when he joined the Air Force and needed his birth certificate.

At that time, he looked at the name listed as his father, and it wasn't the man who he'd always seen as his dad. This led to conversations with his mother regarding the discrepancy, which she has refused to discuss with him. They have discontinued contact due to this issue.

Mike confronted his mom with an ultimatum to help him find his biological father. If she didn't help him, he would tell the man who raised him the truth. His mother didn't comply, which led Mike to speak to the man who raised him about why his name wasn't on his birth certificate. Mike never had the heart to tell him that he wasn't his father and ask him to take a DNA test. He passed away a few years before the interview.

A couple of years before the interview, Mike did an ancestry.com query into his ethnic makeup and connected to his biological father's brother. From there, he was connected to his biological father's family. His biological father passed away when he was 12 years old, so he never got the opportunity to meet him. He met one of his biological father's granddaughters and also one of his nieces who grew up around the corner from where he lived. Mike found out that he has an older sister by ten months, but she hasn't been willing to meet with him due to her love for her father's memory.

Other Role Models

Mike had an uncle, whom he referred to as his "keep it real" uncle. This uncle helped him identify perspectives that he otherwise was unable to find at times. To Mike, he was a positive role model even while watching him make bad decisions. This uncle taught him about safe sex by telling him about the amount of money he loses per check-in child support allotments. His uncle was a positive male influence who saw his potential and helped him to realize it.

Mike has not maintained a relationship with his uncle. Maintaining familial relationships has been a struggle for him throughout his life. The issues with his uncle began when he joined the military. His uncle took umbrage with him joining the "white man's Army." After that, his uncle had an issue with Mike marrying a Puerto Rican woman instead of an African American woman. Mike's grandmother led the way with the bigotry regarding his wife, at times calling her a "dirty Puerto Rican." This situation contributed to the family estrangement and his wife disconnecting from the family. Mike's former favorite uncle is now still living with his mother. He sees him as an example of what a man shouldn't be instead of what a man is.

Impact on Mike the Man

Mike believes that due to his lack of a relationship with his father or any consistent father figure, he was angry a lot. He acted out in school and even recalled biting teachers at a young age. In addition to the anger, he also suffered from low self-esteem issues. During this time, teachers were allowed to "spank" children, and he reacted negatively to that type of punishment.

He also believes that feeling abandoned impacted his relationship decisions as he matured. His first failed marriage resulted from thinking that he'd found someone that could provide him the love that he had sought his entire life. He says that he was naive and too trusting, which led to poor decision-making, that he still suffers.

Mike doesn't believe that there is a direct correlation between not having a father and his divorces. He states that his first divorce resulted from getting married far too young (20 years old). His second marriage failed due to issues that his wife had with his daughter from a previous relationship. Mostly, he says he wasn't able to deal with adversity within the confines of a relationship. The loss of those relationships led to him feeling unlovable.

Growing up the way he did had an impact on Mike's parenting style. Due to not having an example of a good father, he had to learn many lessons independently. In the early stages of parenting, he was a "spanker." As a result, his first reaction to misbehaving was to spank his children. As time went on, he realized that being there for his children was a much better deterrent. He also had a tendency early on to view his children as burdens to deal with instead of blessings. As he grew and matured as a father, that has changed. He also has realized that he can't correct the wrongs of his father through his parenting.

He has learned to talk to his children as "people," which helped him immensely as a parent. They discuss topics relevant to the world around them and keep the door open for their children to learn. He views fatherhood now as a "coach." He tries to give the children a "playbook" that they can use for life.

Being a Role Model

Mike reaches out to others who grew up in similar situations as he grew up in to encourage them to push for their best. He uses his honesty and openness to discuss his story growing up to impact those he meets positively. He views that as one of the qualities that make him a role model to others.

He is not currently active in youth mentoring initiatives, but he worked with the Boys and Girls Club and Big Brother/Big Sister programs when he lived in Utah. He has also coached youth teams in multiple sports. He says that children from 5-8 years old are his favorite age group to work with because they're more malleable than the older kids.

Words for Dad

If Mike could meet and speak to his biological father, he would start by asking him, "Where were you?" After they got beyond that, he would tell his father that he doesn't hold anything against him. He knows that there are two sides to every story, and he's sure that his mother wasn't giving him the whole story. Mike doesn't feel as though his father didn't want him. He'd like to tell his father all about himself and find out everything about his biological father. He'd ask his father to tell him stories from his childhood, so he'd know all there is to know about him. He'd want to ask for advice about being a better father. He knows they can't make up for the lost time, so he'd like to create a better future. He finished this interview by saying that he'd want his father to choose to be a part of his life or don't waste his time. He believes that it's hard to lose what you've never had.

BYRON RAY

Hometown: Columbia, SC
Education Level: Bachelor's Degree (Science and Communication)
Occupation: Parent Advocate (Elementary School)
Married: Yes >1 year
Kids: 2 boys (2, 4)

Byron's father was in his life growing up. His parents were married for over 30 years. Overall, their relationship was good, but it got rocky around his high school years because he wanted his independence. His father was a "man of God" and a military man, so the structure was a significant aspect of their family life. Around Byron's sophomore year of high school, they began to butt heads. His father lost his job, which led to much of his father's frustration as Byron grew into manhood. His father made sure that Byron knew who the man of the house was despite his growing independence and the financial setbacks at the time of his upbringing.

Byron stated that he had a "tremendous fear" of his father growing up. As he got older, he sought approval from his father as opposed to fear. At one point, he dropped out of college and went back to live with his parents. After that setback, he would always call his father to find out what his father thought before deciding. That extended from relationship decisions to job choices and in many different areas of his life.

Good Times

Though Byron noted that he shared so many great times with his father, one story that stood out to him was when his car broke down. He had a habit of buying used cars and trying to fix them on his own. He loved to go to the library and study the manuals for different car models he owned to go back and work on his cars. Byron recalls his father waking him up early in the morning to help him fix other vehicles. Though he didn't want to do it, he realized that this was his father's way of spending time with him, so he'd put on some clothes and help his father. One time that stands out was when his father showed him how to change the oil in his car for the first time. He recalls his father taking out the appropriate tools with, as he described his father having black, greasy hands while wearing a dirty Morehouse sweater and aqua blue sweatpants. He remembers looking at his father and thinking that his father is Superman. He saw that his father didn't have to take his car to shops to get fixed as his superpower. To this day, he takes the approach of doing things for himself instead of having someone else do it for him. He credits his father with that line of thinking, and that has motivated him his whole life.

Superstar

His father would put notes in his lunch box when he was in elementary school. He remembers pulling out his lunch of bologna and cheese sandwich, plain chips, juice, and oatmeal pie to find a note that said, "You are a Superstar!" He would get a message like that every day from his father. His father still calls him "Superstar" to this day, and it's a reminder to him that regardless of the mistakes he may make in his life, his father still thinks he's a superstar.

Other Positive Males

In addition to his father, Byron had other positive males in his life. Byron credited his church family as positive role models that stood in the gap for him in addition to his father. He says that every deacon, minister, and pastor at the church took a role in his life as a mentor. One youth pastor specifically and a contemporary gospel group stood out to him as positive influences.

Being a Dad

Byron's oldest child (5 years old) was working on his writing, and he began crying because it was difficult. He used that opportunity to explain to his son that anything he wanted to accomplish would take hard work. He told him that his father also gave him that message and took pride in sharing that message with his son.

Being a Role Model

In 2008, Byron began mentoring in schools through the WINGS for kids program. He also mentors a young man who lives in his apartment complex. He finds that it's the small things that mean something to the youth, and he uses those opportunities to help young people when he can. Through mentoring, he has realized the change and impact that he can cause through interactions with young people.

Words for Dad

Byron would love to tell his father, "Thank you for taking a chance." Byron's father's father wasn't active in his life, but despite that, Byron's father was great. At the age of 27, Byron called his father to thank him for being a good dad, and Byron's father told him that one of the most thankless jobs you can do is be a father.

Parting Thoughts

Byron's parting thought is, "If you have the chance to impact a young person's life, do it now. Don't make them pay for your absence later. You can change a life."

DENNIS GREEN

Hometown: Ridgeville, SC
Education Level: Bachelor's Degree (Culinary Management)
Occupation: Chef
Married: Yes (10 years)
Kids: 3 (1 daughter (18), 2 sons (10))

Dennis had his father in his life. After his parents' divorce, he lived with his father for some time, in addition to living with his grandparents. He and his father had a good relationship growing up. When he got to high school, he wasn't involved in many extracurricular activities for unknown reasons. Still, as he got older, his father became a "big brother" type figure who would give him information about new things and different things he was interested in. Dennis referred to his family as a "video game" loving family. His father played video games with them. They would also pick up friends to go bowling, to the amusement parks, etc. His father was a "fun dad."

He mostly feared disappointing his father. When necessary, Dennis states that his father would give him a grab and squeeze to let him know that he was serious, but most of this fear related to his father came from not wanting to disappoint him. He tried to make his father proud. He never needed to do anything extra to stand out to his father, but he wanted to impress him.

Other Role Models

Dennis credits his grandfather and his uncles for being role models for him growing up, as well. They were always around doing different activities, going on trips, family cookouts, etc. They had things in common with his father, but some differences gave him a "spider web" of positive males around at all times. This was important because it gave him many different examples of what a successful man was. They were various leaders with other goals, but they were all men he could model himself after and learn. Also, he knew that all of them cared greatly for him, giving him an understanding of love from that standpoint.

Lessons Learned

Dennis has learned to swallow his pride and say what he needs help with from his spouse. He never saw any of this done by any of the males growing up. He realized that this is necessary to maintain a good relationship. He highlights that men didn't see it as "manly" to be vulnerable enough to ask anyone for anything. That also showed in the ways that they treated their wives. He's made a point of allowing himself to be more willing to speak up for his needs and wants in his relationship.

Passing It On

If he could pass one trait from his father to his children, it would be to "hustle" legally. His father was a "jack of all trades" and master of many of them. Being able to hustle gave him many opportunities to do things that others did not. He was always able to provide for his family because of his work ethic.

One trait that he wouldn't pass on to his children from his father would be his money management skills. Managing finances was a struggle for his father. Though he had a knack for hustling to make money, saving money was not his strength. He thought it was okay for him to spend money in abundance because he believed it would be easy for him to make it back.

Being a Role Model

Dennis mentors locally within the Distinguished Gentlemen's Club Mentoring Program. He has two young men in the organization that he works with specifically. He also mentors a few young men in his home church and his natural home mentoring with his sons. Through his job, he also ends up mentoring people that he runs into. He got into it because he wanted to change the world but realized he couldn't do it himself. He wanted to begin with changing himself and then reaching out to young people. He likes young people because they are still moldable and don't hold grudges.

Dennis enjoys passing on the knowledge that he's accumulated over time. He believes that if he gives information to another person about how he's accomplished something, the person he's shared the news with should achieve the same (if not more) in a shorter period than it took him. Being able to invest in young people has the intrinsic gratification that comes with it. He says, "The farmer doesn't know which seeds he plants will grow and bear fruit, but he plants enough to be able to count on a plentiful harvest."

He says that there are times that you realize how much a kid is into the process of being mentored. He recalls taking kids to Carowinds, hockey games, and NBA games and living the experience through the child's eyes.

Words for Dad

Dennis's father passed away a few years ago on a date close to his birthday, and it still affects him. When it gets close to his birthday, he tends to feel down and stay away from family.

If he could say anything to his father, he would tell his father that he "did his part." He was amazing and taught him a lot of things that he needed him to know. He would also tell him that he strives to continue the legacy that his father began. He wants to be a strong man, a good father, and instill the values in his children that his father instilled in him. He said if he saw him, he'd probably just stare at him like a kid on Christmas morning.

Parting Thoughts

"Change the world by changing yourself."

"Show me a successful individual and I'll show you someone who had real positive influences in his or her life. I dont care what you do for a living—if you do it well I'm sure there was someone cheering you on or showing the way. A mentor."

— Denzel Washington

HERBERT JENKINS JR.

Hometown: Charleston, SC
Education Level: High School Graduate and some college
Occupation: Butcher
Married: Yes (9 years), 1 Divorce
Kids: 5 (3 boys, two girls)

Herbert grew up with his father in his home, along with his mom, brothers, and sister. His father and mother were married for 53 years. His father was a truck driver and played in a band, so he was often gone on weekends. Despite his busy schedule, his father encouraged Herbert to talk to him whenever he felt necessary. He would take the opportunity to speak to his dad whenever they had a chance to spend some time together.

Relationship Examples

According to Herbert, his parents had a pretty good relationship. He believed that his mother would allow his father to do whatever he wanted and give him whatever he desired. Despite their primarily positive relationship, domestic violence was something that Herbert witnessed between his father and mother. He would observe his parents fussing or his father choosing to run away. He believes that his father wanted his way, which led to many of the issues with Herb's mother. It was not uncommon for Herbert and his brothers to receive beatings from their dad when they misbehaved.

Impact on Herb the Husband

When Herbert was married to his first wife, he replicated the behavior that he saw from his father while growing up, which included physically abusing his wife. In his second marriage, he has been more considerate of how he can better deal with conflict. He always thought that men ruled and that his wife would have to do whatever he said. He now understands that it is not okay to abuse women, nor should he always have his way.

Becoming a Father

Before becoming a father himself, Herbert says he spent his time "hanging around and doing nothing with his life." When he became a father, it made him want to do more. He didn't want anyone telling him that he needed to take care of his child. He mentioned that his child's mom came to stay with him and his family for a while because her mother would not let him visit her home. This incident motivated him and encouraged him to go out each day and work to support his family.

Herbert's dad ensured that his children were cared for, even if it meant neglecting himself. When he became a father, he adopted the same policy. He says that his goal as a father was to be a role model for his children to teach them how to be independent. He believes his sons have taken this lesson of independence to heart.

Being a Role Model

He believes he is a good role model to his children and other young people he's come into contact with. He, however, has a unique way of mentoring as his method is to guide people to the options they have waiting for them. At that point, the individual can decide what it is they plan on doing with those options. Once he has presented the options, he moves on. Where they wish to go from there is entirely up to them.

When his children think of him, he would want his children to think of love. He realizes that he's not perfect, but he gave his children everything he had to offer. If he had all of his children in a room together, he would tell them to love and respect each other as a family because it is all they have.

Regrets

His greatest regret as a father was that he didn't spend more time with his family. He also says he would've been less stern on his children as they were growing up.

Words for Dad

If Herbert could have one last conversation with his father, he would tell his father that he loved him. He says that's important because his father never said he loved him while he was alive.

CORDARRO BROWN

Hometown: North Charleston, SC
Education Level: High School Graduate
Occupation: Automotive Technician
Married: Yes (9 years)
Kids: 2 daughter, 1 son

Cordarro's father was in his life and lived in his home growing up. His parents weren't married at the time of his conception, but they did get married later. When he was six years old, his parents got divorced.

The divorce of his parents had a significant impact on him. He couldn't understand it and internalized his thoughts and feelings toward it. At that age, he already had the mindset that his parents would always be together. The final straw before the divorce was a massive fight that Cordarro witnessed. The fight hurt him and caused him to have a lot more problems as he got older.

After the divorce, his relationship with his father became almost like a love/hate relationship. When his parents fought, it got physical, and it caused him to view his father differently. His father started going to church and tried to teach him not to put his hands on women. Cordarro had difficulties accepting that message because his mind kept replaying the memories of his parents' fights.

After the divorce, the relationship between his mother and father was rocky. He recalls his parents had to go to court to regain custody of the kids after the divorce. His mother moved to Los Angeles to look for work, while his dad stayed in South Carolina. He and his siblings would go back and forth between them until his mother got a stable job.

Relationship with Dad

Growing up, Cordarro feared his father, but it wasn't the type of fear that he has developed for him today. It was more like a fear of being disciplined. He believes the fear of his father was the healthy kind that kept him from getting in too much trouble. He and his father also shared many positive memories, including going to basketball games and practices together. He and his father now have an excellent relationship. He says that after they both matured in Christ, they have been able to forgive and forget.

Cordarro states that his father made him the man that he is today. He told his father at his 50th birthday party that as long as he could remember, he and his sisters never went without food, never remember the lights being turned off, and they always had clothes on their backs. His father showed him what it meant to be a provider, a protector, and a man in general. He still wishes that he were more affectionate.

Other Positive Males

In addition to his father, Cordarro had other positive male influences. He says that his grandfather played a significant role in allowing him to see the affectionate side of men.

Impact

He says that his relationship with his father contributed to his decision to get married and become a father. He believes that marriage is "God's idea," and God desires men to have children and be fruitful. According to him, "God wants you to lead, protect, and provide." Even though his parents' marriage failed, he realized that there is still life and a chance to move on when marriages don't work out the way you hoped.

Becoming a Father

Though Cordarro tries his best, he sometimes finds himself replicating some of the negative behaviors he saw from his father growing up. He sometimes doesn't show enough affection towards his kids, and he tries to check himself when it happens because it scares him. He states God allows us to do better than what was done before us.

His character, personality, and decision to give his life to Christ has led Cordarro to think of his father as a good man. People often referred to his father as a gentle giant because of how humble he was.

Being A Role Model

Cordarro believes that he is a positive role model based on the countless interactions with people in his church and his family. People often pull him aside or send him a message about his impact on their lives.

He believes in maturity, gratitude, constancy, commitment, passion, and trustworthiness and uses these character traits to live his life.

Cordarro thinks mentoring has impacted his perspective because he sees the younger generation as misguided. He believes that they just need someone to remind them of their worth. He is currently working with some of his younger cousins. He calls and visits them to spend time, hear them out, and give them some good advice.

Words for Dad

In parting, Cordarro would love the opportunity to tell his father, "I love you, and I appreciate you just being here despite the bumps in the road. Just you being there and being consistent has spoken volumes. Your presence has carried into how I am with my kids now."

"JOHNNY PHILLIPS"

Hometown: North Charleston, SC
Education Level: High School Graduate (Currently in College)
Occupation: College Student (Pursuing Degree in Biological Science)
Married: No
Kids: No

Growing up, Johnny's father was in his life intermittently. He would mostly come around when he was in the area for disciplinary reasons. He wasn't in Johnny's life for the most part outside of an occasional weekend visit. He never knew where his father lived, but he recalled visiting a place that his father lived once when he was eight or nine years old.

His father and mother were never married. Johnny was conceived while his mother was in college, which led to her dropping out of college. The relationship didn't work out after the pregnancy, and Johnny's birth father was not present for his birth. His godfather attended his birth.

His godfather served as a positive male role model once Johnny became an adult. He didn't meet his godfather until around his 20th birthday, primarily because he lived in New York. His godfather paid for him to travel to New York for his 20th birthday to meet his father's other son, who was one year older than Johnny.

His mother is now married to his stepfather, whom he didn't consider a positive figure growing up due to chronic alcoholism. He believes that not having a fatherly figure growing up led to some negative issues in his life. He credits his mother and grandmother for being his "rocks" and teaching him what he knows about being a man.

Impact

Johnny believes that being raised by his mother and grandmother led to struggles with relationships with women and not knowing what he thinks a man should know. His work ethic is a result of watching his mom and grandmother work. His mother and grandmother worked extremely hard to make sure that he had what he needed. He learned a lot of what not to do as a man from watching his mom.

He says that he grew up fast in the urban North Charleston, SC area. He wasn't able to see male figures who consistently worked hard growing up. Johnny attributes getting his "backbone" by learning his way through his rough surroundings. Interactions in the neighborhood, schools, etc., allowed him to pick up survival skills that have helped him to this day.

Johnny says that he wasn't the best-behaved student, but he got good grades once he got to high school because he realized how vital academics were. He played football in high school, which gave him access to positive male role models.

Positive Male Role Models

He believes that he learned a lot about work ethic and consistency from football training. His coaches were examples of positive men in his life. He used his ability to watch and learn from people around him to look for positive characteristics. He observed his coaches identify what made them stand out as strong.

Johnny had one coach who motivated the team using passionate speeches. It came out when he was pushing players to be their best. He compared his coaches to people who yell to criticize or tear down. This coach wasn't like that, and because of that, he still maintains a relationship with that coach.

Johnny was also involved in the school band, and he recalls band directors being "cutthroat." In middle school, he was able to go to a better school because of family connections. As one of the only African American students in the school, he stood out, and social stigmas came with the territory. Most of the students came from families that were better off financially than he was. Johnny played the saxophone, but he didn't have the newest instrument, which made him the subject of ridicule at times. His band director would encourage him to get himself together so that he could excel in the band.

Johnny recalls that though he came across positive male role models growing up, none of those have happened to be black. He currently has a mentor who is a Caucasian male. His mentor and wife purchased him a car to get from place to place to recognize his hard work in school.

His mentor is a cardiologist at a well-respected hospital in the Charleston, SC, area. Johnny was introduced to his mentor thanks to his grandmother, who has been their family housekeeper for years. He has considered them family for a long time. Occasionally, Johnny's mentor gives him clothes (they wear the same size). He calls to check in with him and asks him about his future career plans. His mentor also enlisted the help of his doctor friends when Johnny was raising money for a trip. Without their help, he would not have been able to afford to go on the trip.

Once his mentor found out that Johnny was interested in pursuing a career in medicine, he took a vested interest in his steps to achieve this goal. His mentor has encouraged him to be an avid reader and commonly recommends books to check out. He has even allowed Johnny to shadow him at the hospital and interact with patients. There is also another doctor he's come into contact with whom he looks to for professional advice regarding the medical field.

Though Johnny views his mentor as a great professional role model, there are still things that he doesn't discuss with him. Johnny feels there would be awkwardness because his mentor came from such a different background. The mentor's father was a Greek immigrant, and they have experienced racism in the US, but he still doesn't try to engage him in those types of discussions.

Being a Positive Role Model

In many ways, Johnny believes that he is a good role model based on his actions and aspirations. He does admit that he has a lot to learn.

Reflection on His Father

Johnny had a discussion with his father where he told him that he felt as though he could've been a better father. Though he's never been angry about his father's absence in his life, he also realizes that you can't miss what you've never had. According to Johnny, his friends also didn't have their fathers in their lives. As a result, this didn't impact him as much as it would've if he were the only one of his friends who had no relationship with his father.

Johnny admits that his father's father didn't raise him, so he didn't know how to be a father because he didn't have a father. Johnny says that he once told his father that he "at least should've tried" when it came to taking an active role in his life.

Parting Thoughts

Johnny continues to aspire to do great things with his life. He wants to show kids who grew up like him that you can overcome any situation through hard work and a commitment to being great. He refuses to allow himself to accept less than the best from himself. He says Assata Shakur is an inspiration to him because of the things that she endured. Johnny believes that he will be one of the next great inspirations for generations to come.

STEPHAN WHALEY

Hometown: Charleston, SC
Education Level: Bachelors
Occupation: Public School Educator
Married: No
Kids: No

Stephan's father was present until he was nine years old. His father and his mom were having marital issues and separated when he was eight years old and eventually divorced when he was nine. After the divorce, he did not see much of his father until he graduated from high school.

There were a few times when Stephan had contact with his father. His mother would request that he ask his father for money to pay for his high school band trips. His father wasn't paying child support and was also not interested in giving his son anything else.

Impact

Stephan believes that one of the main reasons he clung to specific male figures in his life was due to the absence of his father. His father's absence, however, did make him hold on to particular memories of things he taught him when he was present. Some lessons were good, some bad, and some caused confusion and left him feeling that he was not a worthy son.

Conversations

When he was older and in his late 20's, he had the opportunity to have a conversation with his father. He tried to debunk some of the theories his father taught him. He believes that these conversations were somewhat beneficial but would have been a lot more meaningful if he had imparted this wisdom when he was growing up.

Stephan believes his father influenced his decision to go to college instead of being forced into joining the military instead. He discloses that his father was a very articulate man. He did not attend college and reveled in the fact that he had the intellect of individuals that did go to college.

His father worked in law enforcement and would take extra jobs providing security for basketball and football games. He would take Stephan to see these games whenever he was working. He would also take him to his first-ever Battle of the Bands, where he fell in love with band music.

Different Strokes

Stephan speaks of growing up with his older brother. He made many decisions outside of what their father preferred. His brother still ended up going back to the route their father had suggested in the long run. With his father being absent and his brother six years his senior, Stephan looked up to him a lot when making his own life decisions. He says it was difficult to see his brother not knowing what he wanted to do with his life. His brother didn't have much direction, which made it difficult for Stephan to make decisions. He decided that he would find something that he was good at and would not burden his mother with the debt of putting him through college. He believes that if his father had played a more active role in his life, he would have made decisions differently.

Resentment

Stephan has some slight resentment towards his father. He believes his father made many selfish decisions and often wonders why he never chose him as a priority. When Stephan became involved in the church, he found some positive influence in a particular individual who would mentor boys like himself that did not have a father in their lives.

His brother holds more of a grudge towards their father than he does. He says that once his brother has decided how he feels regarding a situation, that's how it will be.

Other Male Role Models

Eventually, Stephan's mother got remarried. Her husband was heavily involved in the church, and Stephan's father resented this gentleman. There was often fallout between his father and male figures who tried to provide some positivity in his life. This also affected the relationship he and his brother had with these male figures. Stephan's mother's husband would take him and his brother to college football games. He had never experienced that in his life, so he thought it was fantastic. Stephan also mentions his uncle was a positive figure who owned a chauffeuring business. This uncle would teach him things about the company, have him clean the cars, and take him for rides in the limos. He appreciated these gestures as he did not have anyone else around at that time. He says this gave him something else to do rather than sitting around his house and feeling all alone.

Making Daddy Proud

Stephen said that he did many things to make his father proud, especially true of piano recitals and band performances. Stephan took up playing basketball to follow in his brother's and father's footsteps; his father never made it to any of his games. He started playing soccer; his father would miss those games too. His father was not there to see many of his accomplishments. His father missed one key event when he was inducted into the National Honor Society in high school. His father did show up when he graduated from high school and college. Stephan later moved in with his father when he decided to move back to Charleston, SC.

Stephan believes his father was a good man for the most part. He thinks his father compartmentalized his happiness with what he thought were his responsibilities as a father. He considered this to be an arrogant decision. He believes his father laid a good enough foundation with his older brother. His brother was sixteen when he decided to leave home. Stephan believes that his father instilled many positive attributes into his brother and his brother passed them on to him in his father's absence.

Being a Positive Role Model

Stephan tries to be a positive role model by showing the students he encounters daily to be who they are. He says they don't need to be perfect and should be comfortable with who they are. He mentions that his students see parts of him that they don't like. He says that's okay because it will give them the ability to have more respect for him in the long run.

He shares the parts of his life story that he deems are worth sharing with his students. Most of the students during his teaching career could identify with having an absentee father. In contrast, the population he currently teaches can identify with an overbearing, high expectations father.

Stephan does not have kids that he mentors regularly but does provide mentorship whenever opportunities present themselves with students from his past. He appreciates the fact that he can drop a jewel or a kind word whenever they approach him for a conversation. He believes they appreciate knowing that someone from their past will still send them a message now and again. He thinks it is essential for them to feel like there is still someone in their corner.

Words for Dad

There are so many things Stephan would like to say to his father if he were given the opportunity. Among those things is letting him know that the sacrifices he made, and the amount of work he put in, were enough. This would contradict what he taught his sons because they were taught to excel and not be mediocre and lazy. This is where he believes his father fell short. His father did succeed in teaching them how to be better men than he was.

Stephan's father taught them how to decide that they can live with and not be influenced by other people. That way, if they are unsuccessful, they can blame no one but themselves. He taught them that making a decision based on somebody else meant the world too consumed them. He knows that his father had regrets. His father made his decisions for himself, and he had to live with the outcomes. Stephan feels that he was comfortable with his life choices.

Parting Thoughts

Stephan says that he has a story about personal growth thanks to his life lessons and how he has used absence to motivate his life. The lack of someone from your life does not mean a closed-door or the end of things to come. It is a way to write your own story and build character as you learn to cherish relationships.

He thinks many men are lost because they did not have solid male relationships. This starts with lacking a relationship with their parents. For this reason, he found himself clinging to and learning from men who were older and more experienced than he was.

He believes that not having your father around leaves an opening for someone else to see the greatness in you. He thinks you just have to be open to receiving that attention and cultivating that relationship. It might not be a family member, but it will be someone who has the same amount of love to give you. When your energy is pure, people can sense that and want to be a part of your life.

VINCENIO DAWKINS SR.

Hometown: Akron, OH
Education Level: Associates Degree
Occupation: Salesperson
Married: Yes (4 years)
Kids: 3 (2 girls aged 3 and 7 years), (1 boy age 1 year), and another daughter who is not his biologically

For the most part, Vincenio's father was a part of his life but wasn't a consistent presence. His mother and father were never married. Not having his father in his life was something that he didn't realize impacted him as a child, but his opinions have changed as he has gotten older. His father was out of his life for roughly four years due to moving to California to pursue job opportunities. Those years were a critical time in his life (middle to high school) where he was learning about girls, and peer pressure began to kick in. For him, those four years were a big deal and something that he looks back on and realizes made a difference in who he is today. He says that his father was a positive role model in his life despite a few negative aspects. His father had a positive influence on him when he had the opportunity to be around.

Other Positive Men

Vincenio had a stepfather who stepped into the fatherly role. His uncle and sports coaches were other men whom he admired. The men who were role models stood out because they were black men who exemplified the standards of what a man should be. They spent time with him, talked to him, and encouraged him.

He got into sports because he was always around it as a child. His father was into sports, and he also played it as a hobby with his friends. His sports of choice were track and field, football, and basketball.

His stepfather was the person who always encouraged him to do better in school, treating athletics, and life. He also taught him about perseverance, how a man should carry himself, overcome obstacles, maintain a positive attitude, and take things seriously.

Unlike many kids who felt they didn't want another man taking their father's place, he remembers wanting a stepfather. At first, he was reluctant to accept him, but once he realized that he was there to help him, he latched on. They still have a positive relationship, even after he divorced his mother. He still calls his stepfather every year to tell him Happy Father's Day.

Relationship Observations as a Child

Even though his stepfather was a positive influence in his life, he wasn't necessarily the best example of how to treat the women you love. He remembers arguments between his mother and stepfather that he thought were disrespectful to his mother and children. Due to infidelity on his part, their marriage ended. He recalls feeling let down when he found out because he looked up to his stepfather.

Relationship with Biological Father

Vincenio and his father have maintained a positive relationship though he doesn't speak to him as much as he talks to his mom. His relationship with his mother has always been closer because he was an only child. Talking about feelings is not an option with his father. He said, "Often, fathers, especially old-fashioned/old schooled fathers, think that their role is to provide for their children and teach them 'manly' things. That's what my dad taught me. I learned many things about working, responsibility, and other stuff. But at the same time, we never talked about any emotions and feelings."

He continues, "What's crazy is still to this day; if I have something like that to talk about, I don't bring it to my dad. First of all, I'm probably not that comfortable because I've never really had that type of conversation with him. I never communicated with him on that type of level. Secondly, he has a temper. I think he controls it a lot better now. As a result, I just don't feel comfortable sharing some things with him to this day just because he wasn't there for me in that capacity back then."

Good times

Vincenio considers his stepfather was the number one role model for the relationship he had with his kids. "He might not have been the best example as far as female relationships, but his relationship with his kids is pretty good."

He was always there for him during good and bad times. They would have conversations of substance and not just talk about sports all the time. They spoke about the future and what he planned on doing when he grew up. He was always a straight shooter as well. If I said I wanted to do something, he would tell me to look at what I was doing currently in my life and see if that would result in having the future that I wanted. Often it didn't.

He thinks as a father figure, it's not so much beating down on someone verbally, but at the same time checking them and getting them back in line. That's what he did for me. Even if I didn't appreciate it at the time, he was right most of the time."

Being a Father

Vincenio has multiple children, but one of his daughters is biologically not his. The child's father is still in her life. "The backstory with him and my wife is that they never worked out, and shortly after 'my daughter' was born, he exited the picture. My wife then pretty much raised her alone until I entered the picture when she was two years old."

Once her father started seeing how involved Vincenio was with her and that his wife no longer needed his support, her father tried to cause rifts in their relationship. At the time of this interview, they were in a custody battle seeking sole custody. He believes that all this transpired because he recognized that there was now a positive role model in his daughter's life, and he felt some guilt for not being present in her life.

The Impact of His Examples on Being a Father

He says that he emulated certain things that he observed by spending time with the positive role models he had growing up. He also registered some of the negative experiences he had with his father and made a mental note not to repeat those actions based on how they affected him. These are the qualities that have helped him to be a better father.

Vincenio learned many good things from different people he was around growing up and tried to emulate them. He believes the most significant part of him being a good father is his relationship with God and practicing what the Bible says about being a father and being a man of God at all times.

Showing Emotions

He admits that he tries to incorporate emotional feedback when dealing with his children, but it's also something that he needs to work on. "My mom and I can talk about anything, like the most profound darkest stuff. But at the same time, my mom wasn't affectionate with me. I can talk to my kids on any level and don't have a problem. But I think sometimes I have a problem showing affection with my children, and I didn't understand it until my wife brought it to my attention."

He says that he did not have the same type of relationship as a typical family when it came to affection. He doesn't think it was due to a lack of love from his mother. Instead, he attributes it to the amount of work it took to support their household as a single mom.

Being a Mentor

Vincenio is a mentor in his local community. He says, "There are a couple of reasons why I mentor, the most important reason being I feel like it's my purpose in life. It doesn't feel like a job for me. I gain joy in it, whether I'm out of pocket or spending time that I don't think I have. I feel a self-reward for that because I am fulfilling my purpose, and I like to help other people."

He continues by saying, "The other reason is that people did it for me. I had people who were not my father, who were still there for me. I learned critical life lessons from them. So I just want to be what they were to me. I had the luxury of having positive male role models, coaches, and mentors. If I hadn't had them, my life could have easily turned out very differently. I like to think that I am on a successful path. Without those positive male figures, I could have easily been lost."

Vincenio says, "For those reasons, I believe I am blessed. When my cup gets filled, I like to serve other peoples' cups because that works.

You pay it forward. I also provide mentorship because I feel that it is my purpose. That is what I see myself doing for the rest of my life."

He continues by saying, "I like to have an open line of communication, and I have to understand where that child is in their life. I want them to know about me, and I want to know about them. I want to build rapport and trust. Having an open communication line gives them an avenue to direct their questions and vent their frustrations. I like to expose them to diversity and situations that I wasn't exposed to.

Vincenio says, "I came from a predominantly black area in Akron, Ohio. My high school probably had five white kids. A lot of people, even in this day and age, have a very closed mentality. All they know is from what their perspective is, and they haven't been anywhere else. Once you get exposed to different environments, you see the world in another way."

He says, "That's what I want to explain to the kids I mentor because some of the kids that I work with now are in the same predicament that I grew up in. They live in a specific neighborhood and have particular financial struggles. All they know is based on just what they have experienced. I want to tell them that it can be better than that. You don't have just to aspire to be a professional basketball player. You can be a doctor, a teacher, or anything you set your mind to. I just want them to know the depths of society and what is available to them in this big world."

He continues, "I like to teach them how to give back to society. Once they can emulate and do what you've taught them, you have reached the point of success. It is important to teach them and see if they can demonstrate what you've taught them. So I give back, and I want to see them give back as well."

Vincenio says, "I just want to be there for them in every aspect of their lives. I shared that my father wasn't there for me emotionally, and I want to be there for them emotionally. I want to have fun with them. We like playing in the yard, playing some football, and stuff like that. I want to be there to provide spiritual guidance. It's not just about being there in the moment. When I mentor, I am there for that child for the rest of their life. As we know, many relationships don't last for the rest of your life, but I want to be that constant positive person that's always there for them. Sometimes people only come for a season, and if that's what they need me for, that's fine. If they need me 20 years down the road, that's fine. I still want to be that old guy who has some wisdom to give to them."

It has always been Vincenio's passion to help other people. He is keen on assisting youth because this is the time when bad habits are learned, and acceptable practices are formed. Many people within his age group and younger did not have that kind of guidance growing up, and he wants to foster positive male relationships. There are many single-parent homes, and there is a lot that a mother cannot teach her son about being a man. He would love to fill the void in some of these households where a father figure is not present.

He finds being a mentor very rewarding, and children have personally thanked him for his Impact Program. They are eager to attend the next meeting, and their parents have noticed the positive changes in their children because of this program.

Vincenio got into mentoring because he saw a program in North Dakota called The Boys Club. That program is similar to the model he is currently providing through the Impact Program. From that model, he created the structure for what he wanted to do. He wanted to treat these boys to field trips and activities, but he also wanted to add a more personal touch to it, such as having opportunities for one-on-one private discussions.

Vincenio feels it is his duty to be a mentor. Many people complain about how things are, but they don't come up with a solution. He did not want to be one of those people. He believes that if these kids were exposed to something other than what they were used to and had a positive outlet, things would change.

Vincenio states, "I believe I am a positive role model because I feel like I have learned from other people's mistakes. I've learned from my own mistakes, my father's mistakes, and other role models' mistakes. Also, I get a lot of compliments on how I am raising my children. In my heart, I feel like I am going about life the right way."

OMAR MUHAMMAD

Hometown: Augusta, GA
Education Level: Bachelor's Degree in Biology
Occupation: Marine Biologist
Married: Yes (15 years) (No divorce)
Kids: 1 boy (10 years old)

Omar's father was in his life, and their relationship was more traditional in that he was the old-school type of father who didn't necessarily show emotion. The way that he "showed that he loved you" was by taking care of his family. He put food on the table, clothes on their backs, etc., but he didn't necessarily express affection.

Outside of when Omar got in trouble, he didn't fear his father. His father was not the type to "whoop" his kids very often, but he was stern when necessary.

Relationship Observations

His father and mother have been married for around 43 years and are not divorced. Omar remembers that his father treated his mother well. He didn't recall his parents arguing in front of him. They also never showed much emotion in front of the children. They never showed affection in front of the kids either. He could tell that they had love and respect for one another through their interactions. Omar takes pride in not stepping out on his wife, which his father was also serious about.

Fatherly Support

Omar's father cultivated his love of science. His father supported him by purchasing a scientific encyclopedia and helping him with his science projects. He always encouraged him to build on his love of science. His father was supportive of all of his children in this way. Omar's brother was into sports, and their father supported him much in the same way. He never tried to push his sons to do anything that they didn't want to do. Omar remarked that one of the worst things a parent can do is try to force their children into something they aren't interested in.

Omar had a few male teachers that he viewed as role models who helped him stay on the right track. Omar recalls a time where he was participating in a regional science fair, and he experienced racism for the first time. He had created a laser, which was a favorite of the people at the event. The judges didn't choose him as the winner, and he was distraught. He expressed to his father that he didn't want to do science anymore, and his father encouraged him to keep pursuing his love of science. He told him that he could not let those people stop him from doing what he loved. To this day, he is still involved heavily with science and scientific conferences, and in most cases, he is the only African American at those events. He thinks of his father when people have comments or things to say that is negative about his race or religion.

Becoming a Father

Omar says that he parents his son much in the way that his father parented him. Though his wife thinks he should be a little tougher on his son, he takes the more laid-back approach as it pertains to him. He takes the time to speak to his son when he makes mistakes instead of flying off the handle.

Being a Positive Role Model

Omar believes that the way he carries himself and treats people makes him a positive role model. He says that people watch what you do over time more than they listen to what you say. People have come up to Omar and told him that he was "different" based on the conversations that he engages in.

Omar has been mentoring since high school. He started out mentoring at the local library, helping kids with their science and math. When he went to college, he tutored high school students. He took a role in helping college students get adjusted to college life. He's naturally a father to his son, and he's also a guardian ad-litem for foster children.

Omar loves knowing that he helps children make better decisions for their future. He enjoys assisting children in finding other ways to do things and watching them achieve their goals.

Words for His Father

If he could say anything to his father, Omar would say, "Thank you. Thank you for raising me to be the man that I am today. Without you, I know that I would be dead or in jail." Omar's neighborhood had some rough edges that could've led him down a path to destruction, but his father's actions kept him on the right track. Even though his brother got into some trouble, his father did everything he could to help both him and his brother stay on the right path.

CHRIS BEAN

Hometown: Savannah, GA
Education Level: Associate Degrees, Pursuing Bachelor's Degree
Occupation: Military
Married: Yes (6 1/2 years)
Kids: 1 (Boy aged 5)

Chris shares that his father was not in his life growing up. His father chose not to be a part of his life after divorcing his mother before his birth. He did, however, have a stepfather who was around until he was 14 years old.

Impact

Not having a biological father around affected Chris because he had many questions after realizing that he had a different last name from his mother, brother, and step-father. He wondered how it is that a father could have chosen to abandon his child.

Finding Dad

Chris searched in December of 2011, where he successfully made contact with his father. He mailed a letter asking him to reach out if he was his biological father. It was an awkward moment for Chris as his father went through some struggles and wanted to visit his house. This visit was not something Chris was ready for, and after expressing his concerns, his father again disappeared. Chris did make another attempt to find him and instead found an obituary marking his death a few years later.

At first, Chris thought that he had missed an opportunity but then realized that it was his father who had missed out as Chris had achieved many great things. He had a great family, including his wife and son, and had done all this without him. The more he thought about it, the more he realized that living with regret was not an example he wanted to set for his son, and it was his father's regret for not making an effort. What also helped him get over this was the presence of other male figures in his life that he could look up to and seek out for advice.

If he had the opportunity to speak with his father again, Chris would ask what he would do if he could do it all over again. He would also want to share some advice with him, think about the positive things that he could do for his child, how his child could change his life, and think about his impact on someone else's life.

Reflecting on Biological Father

Chris wants his biological father to know that he is a loyal husband and father, a family man. He puts his heart and soul into everything he does, and that he is a man of faith who puts his trust in Jesus Christ and does all he has done for his family.

Chris feels that if his father had been around, there would have been more accountability for his actions during his late teens and early twenties. He mentioned that he was very naive and would do whatever everyone else was doing. There was no permanent male figure to keep him in check, and as his mother was very passive, she would allow him to do whatever he wanted to do as long as he wasn't doing drugs or committing crimes.

Becoming a Husband and Father

Chris thinks that his dedication to his family is absolutely a direct response to his biological father's absence in his life. Both Chris and his wife grew up in broken homes and made a promise to each other when they got married that they would not replay the same scenario within their home and cause it to impact their son's life as it had impacted their lives. They both decided that no matter how challenging situations would get, they would work it out and make the best life for their son. Chris and his wife feel no matter how much pain it caused to them, or if their ignorance got in the way, having a child and being married was more significant than their selfishness.

At home, Chris spends as much time as he can with his son. He mentions that fatherhood and parenting are not the same, and he raises his son in a structured and disciplined environment. He and his wife do not speak negatively to each other or around their son and try to remain positive to see them together as a happy family.

Other "Role Models"

There were more negatives than positives in the relationship between Chris and his step-father. Growing up, he was an obese child, and this caused his step-father to pick on him and call him names such as "Fatty fatty, two by four, couldn't get through the bathroom door." He did, however, contribute some positives to Chris's life, such as discipline and structure, which continue to influence him up to this day. Chris did, however, mention that his grandfather was a positive influence during his childhood.

Chris's step-father kept in contact with his brother. He went on to share a story of what happened when his step-father left them at Christmastime. His mother had bought him a pair of FILA "Grant Hill" shoes as a Christmas gift. On Christmas morning, his mother realized that the step-father, who also wore the same size shoes, had not only left the family, but he had taken the new pair of shoes with him as well. He and his brother still talk about the petty things their step-father would do back then and ask themselves if they would ever do something like that.

Chris's grandfather was a positive influence because he was willing to take the time to show him things and to cultivate him into the man he is now. In the absence of his step-father not showing him or teaching him something, his grandfather taught him how to use his hands, how to fish, how to use tools, how to work on trucks and tractors, and how to use them to grow vegetables. His grandfather would also take him and his brother to see a movie or just to drive around. He filled an empty void for Chris and his brother and groomed them into young adults.

Lessons from Grandpa

Chris's grandfather taught him many things. One trait Chris said he would like to pass on to his son is loyalty. He also mentioned that his grandfather was faithful, especially to his grandmother, and never committed adultery during their marriage. He also said that his grandfather was a hard worker. Chris's grandfather passed away in January of 2013.

Chris believes he is a positive influence in his work and his family life. He has worked for some very abrasive and unapproachable people in the past at work. He deals with this by keeping the lines of communication open and tries to be approachable to the six members of staff whom he supervises. He gets involved with all aspects of the job and frequently checks on them to see how they are doing.

Being a Positive Role Model

Chris provides mentorship to both teenagers and adults alike. He does this through the church and at work and will offer help and conversation if someone needs a person to talk to. In his opinion, there is no such thing as 'I don't have time, so he does his best to make time for those who need his help.

Chris believes that many young men and boys come from broken homes without a father or a positive father figure. He thinks it is our job as men to take them and teach and engage them to prepare them for the future. He mentioned that if we as men do a great job of grooming in this fashion, we will all have a great future.

Illustration: Cedric Tolliver II

"I've learned that people
will forget what you
said, people will forget
what you did, but people
will never forget how
you made them feel."

– Maya Angelou

KEVIN RASBERRY

Hometown: Orangeburg, SC
Education Level: Bachelor's Degree in Psychology and Business Administration, Master's Degree (MBA)
Occupation: Business Owner
Married: Married (5 years), 2 previous marriages (1 annulled)
Kids: 4 biological children (3 boys, 1 girl) 2 stepchildren (1 boy, 1 girl)

Kevin's parents were married for 35 years until both of them passed away. He grew up in the home with his father present. His relationship with his father was great. Kevin recalls following his father everywhere he went as a child. He says there was always a "fear" of not doing the right thing in his household when he was a child. Outside of that, he did not have a fear of his father.

Making Daddy Proud

Kevin always wanted to be like his dad, so there were times that he would go above and beyond to make his father proud. However, the older he got, the more he realized that he didn't have to do anything extra. His father loved him because of who he was, and nothing he did or didn't do would change that.

His father was an auto-body worker for 40 years, and Kevin would help sand cars and sweep around to help. He struggled academically, and being around his dad helped him to develop abilities in other areas of his life.

Kevin played sports, and his father wasn't able to attend his games due to his work schedule. There was always a sense of love between them. He always felt that his parents worked hard to get him what he needed.

Impact

Kevin believed his father had a profound impact on his life. He directly credits his father's influence on his decision to found the first single-gender public school in the state of South Carolina. His father emphasized the importance of mentorship and the need to help and give to others.

This social school was designed to expose young men to literacy, culture, business, and many more life areas. Another emphasis of the school was to provide choices to young men who otherwise may not have had those opportunities. The school's student composition was 97% African American and 98% from poverty-stricken homes.

It lasted three years, and he took great pride in opening and running that school.

Other Positive Role Models

Kevin's best friend's father was like a father to him, and a great deal of the men in the neighborhood took an active role in his life as a mentor of sorts. The men at his school were also friends of his parents. He estimates that at least 20 men had a positive influence on him.

Kevin has fond memories of interactions with positive males in his life. One day, his dad wasn't around, but he was in an area where many people knew him. Everyone spoke about how good of a man his dad was, and it showed in many different areas of his life. His father showed him that "your character should show up before you do." This instance was an example of his father living the life that he wanted Kevin to live.

Being a Mentor

Kevin still mentors many young men who went to the school. He has assembled a mentor program in the Columbia, SC, area called the Carolina Legacy Council. Many of the young men that he worked with while running the school have joined the program.

All of his life, people poured into Kevin. It's impossible to be around giving your whole life and not want to give back. He finds giving comes naturally and is a requirement in his life. He says that it's who he is meant to be.

Kevin has a quote that he lives by every day. "The manifestation of a man is a direct result of how much he has invested in himself." "What you don't put into you, you don't have to operate from. Become a sponge." He used education and literacy to help other people.

Words for Dad

If he could say anything to his father now, he would tell his father thank you and that he knows that he never told him a lie. Kevin appreciated his father's integrity when it came to him. His honesty when speaking to Kevin was integral to him becoming the man he is today. His father prepared him for life. Kevin would say, "I appreciated your integrity. By instilling it in me, you helped me live with integrity and instill it in other people.

THOMAS CHISOLM

Hometown: Charleston, SC
Education Level: Associate Degree
Occupation: Machine Operator
Married: Yes (1 year), 1 Divorce (9 years)
Kids: 4 (3 girls, 1 boy)

Thomas did not grow up with his father and only had one diminished memory of him when he was two years old, and his father tried to explain the reason for squeezing toothpaste from the back to the front. Outside of this memory, he does not remember anything else about his father.

Impact

He was affected a great deal by his father's absence. He believes that things he could have done differently in the earlier stages of his life had his father being present. He missed out on having his father teach him things such as telling the truth, looking people in the eye, giving a firm handshake, how to pump gas, and how to open doors, to name a few. He notes that it is obvious he missed these lessons as he is not a chivalrous person and had no grooming. His father's absence also left him with questions about himself, his behavior, and his looks. Thomas is now 38 years old and still has unanswered questions.

Questions Linger

Thomas does not know for sure if his father is alive. His last known address was in Columbia, South Carolina, and for all intents and purposes, he could still be living there. He has done some unsuccessful searching on the internet. Thomas was able to get some background information on his father from his aunts, who informed him that his father was a law student and was attending law school when he and his mother were together. His father had planned to get married, but he isn't sure what happened with those plans as they never tied the knot. From this information, Thomas was able to identify certain traits that he inherited from his father, such as his critical and analytical thinking and his love for reading.

Thomas is thankful that God could bring him to a place where he would not be the child who blames their life's achievements, or the lack thereof, on the absence of his father. He hopes that they will one-day cross paths, which he looks forward to.

Words for His Father

Thomas would like to tell his father that he completely understands the decisions he made. He has also made decisions in the past to try and please people, but it all comes down to living his life at the end of the day. Thomas understands the need to live a comfortable life for oneself and the need to bless other people's lives. He would let his father know that there was no need to explain what happened in the past and that it was okay to start from where they are and go from there.

He shares that he probably would have felt differently 16 years ago, but until you become a man, you will never fully understand what it is to be a man. He says, "No matter the number of books or articles you read until the reality becomes yours, you will never know how you will respond." To his father, he would say, "Hey man, I love you. Let's be together."

Other Male Role Models

While Thomas did not have his father, he mentions his uncles (his mother's three brothers) were involved in his life. From her eldest brother, he learned work ethic. He was taught to do things to the best of his ability no matter how minute the job might be, and this is a lesson that he practices to this day. He also found positivity in his grandfather. They lived with him in the late 60s and early 70s. During this time, he was charged with grooming the preachers at his church. His grandfather would teach theology, and he would teach them how to act and carry themselves as Christians. Thomas would not substitute these lessons for the world. They have helped him a great deal in life and taught him how to do things the Christian way and be there for his family.

Being a Positive Role Model

Thomas believes he is a positive role model as he continuously works hard every day to be better than he was the day before. 'Today might not be a good day, but I know there's another day coming, and if I live to see that day, I will make it better than it was today.' He believes that this is what it means to be positive. As long as you live your best life, not causing any trouble, and putting your life in order, you can be nothing else but positive.

With all that life has thrown at him, he believes that God has blessed him to meet people and learn things independently. In a time when positive male figures are slim to none, he is thankful for the opportunity of being able to consider himself as one.

Parting Thoughts

He says, "Living a long life doesn't necessarily make you a man. What makes you a man is the ability to do what God brings you here to do. Until you can fulfill that responsibility or at least start, you have not yet moved into manhood."

He continues, "Being a man is the most challenging job in the world, despite what women might think. It is the hardest thing to do, but it is very doable. If you have never had a physical father, God is always a great example to follow. By not having my biological father around, I have followed God's standards as closely as possible. God may not be happy with me now, but he will be in the end. If I have done what He has tasked me to do, I have done all I have needed to do."

"As far as being a man is concerned, it's all about measuring up to what God says a man is. Everything after that will fall into place. For those who don't have fathers, find a father figure you can look up to. If you are a father and still trying to figure your way through manhood, take your time, it will come. For those who are yet to have their first child, always be ready to learn and always be ready to teach when that time comes. You can never really understand what it is to be a father until you become a father. With these guidelines, you can't go wrong."

"SHAWN BROUGHTON"

Hometown: Bamberg, SC
Education Level: Masters Degree
Occupation: Educator
Married: Yes (11 years)
Children: Yes (3 girls)

Shawn's father was in his life until he was ten years old. His parents had an abusive relationship and were eventually separated, which then led to a divorce. After offering her a place to stay, his mother then moved in with Shawn's Godfather, his father's first cousin.

After the move, his father stopped spending as much time as he used to with him, although he lived only a mere five miles away. He was not active in his son's life, and Shawn would visit his father every other weekend.

Other Role Models

Most of what he learned growing up was taught to him by his Godfather because he immediately took on the fatherly role. His Godfather was a brick mason and taught him the trade and taught him about being a man. Shawn feels that if he had been around his father for a longer time, his pathway in life might have been different. His father had an engineering degree and was very good with computers and cars. Shawn thinks that his father would have probably passed on a few lessons to him. Although his father was somewhat present, his father missed many opportunities to be present in Shawn's life. At one point, his father's visits were reduced to once per month or longer. Shawn played football, and this would occasionally coincide with visitations. Sometimes his father would attend his games.

Shawn's Godfather taught him a few things about being a positive role model and being a man of his word. He also taught him the value of a dollar, as he would take him on jobs and pay him the same wages as he did the older men. There were some negatives to growing up with his Godfather. His Godfather owned a club that would expose Shawn to the type of people who smoked and drank. He admits he would occasionally sneak cigarettes and liquor shots during his time at the club.

Shawn says that he never yearned for any specific kind of attention from his father as his mom provided everything he needed. She worked three jobs, attended all of his minor league games, and coached his teams when she could. There was some jealousy towards his friends who would have their fathers around to spend time with them and do all the things his mother had to be doing, but he understood that his mother was trying to do the best she could to play both roles. His Godfather would step in when necessary to do the best he could do for him.

Shawn remembers a conversation with his wife while visiting his father's house during a wake for a family member. 'You see your dad, and you just talk to him. Meanwhile, you see your Godfather, and you light up. It's like he's fathering you; you're happy to be seeing him.' 'You can tell your relationship with him is a much more loving relationship than what it was with your dad. It's not like you hate him, but you're not happy to see him when you see him.' Shawn never really saw things this way until she brought it to his attention.

Conversations

He spoke of when his father admitted his regret for the things that he had done to his mom, that she did not deserve it, and wished that he had treated her better. His father did not share many details, and he only hoped that his father would have elaborated on incidents to explain why they happened. Those answers were critical because his mother had passed away two years prior from cancer. His father never did respond but instead walked away. He never brought it up again, and Shawn doesn't think he ever will.

Reflections

Shawn held no malice or ill will towards his father. He understood that he wanted to be a dad to him. Since the relationship between his dad and his mom was strained, opportunities did not happen very often where they could get together. His mother would say negative things about his father but, in the same breath, did not restrict him from visiting his father. His mother shared stories of all the bad things that he had done to her in the past. These stories painted him in a bad light. The stories she told were not lies, but Shawn believes she shared this information to cause him to feel the same pain and hatred towards his father. His mother would always say, 'don't you grow up to be like your daddy.' Although she shared these stories, she never once told him that he could not visit his father or that his father could not pick him up.

Shawn did not like the things his father caused to happen with his mom and wished that those incidents never happened. He also never understood how his mom could teach him the lesson of 'forgive and be a loving person but could not let go of the past between herself and his father. He said, "I guess it was hard for her to let it go because it happened to her."

Relationship Observations

Shawn grew up seeing his father controlling the narrative regarding his relationship with women. His father prefers a submissive woman. His father does not think men should share household chores because this is the woman's sole responsibility in the house. This was one reason his father and mom did not get along, as his mother was an educated woman and would speak her mind. She would let him know whenever he was wrong and that she would not be the only one working. He would expect her to come home to cook, clean, and take care of the house after a full day's work.

His father was abusive toward his wife, and Shawn observed his father hitting his mom a few times, but most of the abuse was seen by his sister. There were arguments between his parents, and on one particular occasion, his father hit his mom with a rollerblade. There was also some infidelity from his father, and then he moved on to doing cocaine and smoking weed.

He doesn't think his father was overall a misguided person as they did have some good days. He just feels that his father made some bad decisions. Shawn expressed he wished his father had treated his mother better.

Impact of His Experiences

Shawn has never felt the need to express that he needed his father to be present in his life. He knows that he is far from perfect. He has grown into a good person and does right by his kids. On the other hand, his mom dealt with a lot of stress trying to pull off the roles of mother and father. He believes that if his father was a better husband to his mom, he would be a better husband to his wife and struggle less with being emotionally connected.

His wife often complains that he does not show emotions like saying I love you or through a kiss and the occasional bouquet. He believes that this is hard for him as it is not something he grew up seeing. Shawn saw a man show a woman emotion through the context of sexual desire. He says that he's grateful that he has a wife that understands him and understands that there will be days when he falls short. He believes that if he had grown up knowing how to treat a woman, his relationship with his wife would be better.

Words for His Father

If he could ask his father anything, it would be 'why?' He realizes that his father wasn't in a good place in his life at the time and was going through other stuff.

Becoming a Father

Missing out on love growing up gave Shawn a lot to learn as a family man himself. He stated, "I had to learn how to be a good father and husband." This is something he struggles with as he is who he is based on his life experiences. He takes away a little of every occasion he has had with his father, Godfather, and other male role models and uses that to be the best dad that he can be. Often, he tries to give his kids the love and attention that he wished he had. He makes it a point of duty to be involved and spend time with them as he believes this is time that, once lost, can never be regained. He says, "I make it a point to be a good dad, to love them, to hug them, to show them that I care just to be the best that I can."

He doesn't think his father was a bad dad, especially when he was younger. He bought them a lot of material things, and they lived an upper-middle-class life. All this changed when his parents separated. This is also an issue he has identified within himself as he is always buying his kids a lot of stuff they don't need. Since this is what he grew up with, this is the method he uses for showing love.

Being a Positive Role Model

Shawn is an educator and encounters students that do not have a father figure in their lives. Shawn and his friend started a small mentorship organization a few years ago as a mentor at heart. By looking at the demographics of the children he taught, he would see no name listed under father or a name listed for a father who resides outside of the family home. He would also see a father's name, but the child would express that the named person was not involved in their life when asked. He would be a father in name only.

Shawn tries to mentor these kids and talk to them about the difference between good and evil, what to do and what not to do, as these are conversations he thinks are lacking within their households. He remembers when he coached a football team and told the kids, "I love you." They would often respond that he was gay. This made him realize that these kids were not exposed to unconditional love and did not understand how it felt.

Mentoring these kids is a way for Shawn to make as big a difference as possible by having a consistent and constant relationship with them. Relating to them, understanding where they are coming from, and incorporating discipline is showing unconditional love. These are some of the reasons why he wanted to become an educator in the first place.

DANTE PELZER

Hometown: Charleston, SC
Education Level: Ph.D. Doctorate
Occupation: Higher Education Professional
Married: Yes (8 years)
Kids: 1 (Girl aged 2)

Dante and his father did not have a very close relationship, and he only had a few spontaneous encounters with his father. He remembers getting a phone call or a visit on several birthdays. His father was a trucker and was always on the road, which meant the holidays were never prolonged or overnight.

His father's visits never felt genuine, as his father did a yearly check-in for an hour to give him money. He mentioned some malcontent between his father and mother as his father lived close to them but was not active in his life. As Dante grew older, the visits became fewer. His father did not attend any of his graduations. Dante's father accepted his invitation to his wedding only to show up after the ceremony ended, and the bride and groom exited the chapel.

Dante's father did not provide any financial support for his mother until he began to pay his back child support when Dante was in high school. Until then, he and his mother resided with his grandmother for most of his childhood. His mother would work two jobs to support them financially. When he started the fifth grade, he and his mom moved into low-income housing close to his grandmother, with whom he would stay until his mother had finished working at her second job.

Impact on Dante the Father

Dante wanted to be the opposite of what his father was to him, especially when he became a father. It's been a critical area of focus for Dante regarding his interactions between himself and his daughter. Being engaged and active with his daughter is effortless; being a good father is subconscious and comes naturally.

He does often wonder how a father could abandon and not have a love for his child. For Dante, it was a magical feeling seeing his child being born. To him, that is the purest form of love; the love of a parent to a child.

Dante does not believe his father deserves any credit for wanting to be a better father because of the lack of a relationship with him. Through his absence, he learned how to be loving, considerate, compassionate, and demonstrate love. These lessons have become ingrained in his subconscious and have helped him become the man he is today, and have impacted his interactions with his daughter. However, he acknowledges that how he has turned out is a by-product of that absence from his father.

Words for His Father

If Dante had the opportunity to have an open conversation with his father, he would tell him that he messed up and missed out on seeing an amazing young man grow up and that he missed out on having a great relationship with someone who turned out pretty good. He would tell him that he is okay and that his absence is not a detriment to him as he has found a father in Jesus, in God, and he is okay as he is covered. He would also tell him that he is unfazed and does not need reconciliation.

Dante mentioned that he has spoken to his father a few times but has never had a heart-to-heart with him where he opened up to tell him these things. He would be only direct based on the conversations that they were having. Now, his father only crosses his mind during discussions with his father's sister, who he learned of during grad school. It is through these conversations that he knows what is going on in his father's life. Without these conversations, his father would simply exist, and he would not know.

Other Male "Role Models"

Dante had no immediate male family members who played positive role models. Most of them were either into drug dealing or just examples of bad men. However, one uncle from the military, his favorite uncle growing up, was a good role model until high school. This positive presence did not last too long as the uncle seemed to have changed after returning home from the military. No one knew what happened to him while being there, but he was no longer the same.

Throughout his high school years, Dante found positivity in his history teacher, who he identifies as the first actual positive male figure who inspired him to get involved and do great things. He took honors history, which introduced him to this particular teacher's class. The teacher taught him to debate, which led to Dante's participation in a community service project for elementary kids. He did this for three years which led him to further acting roles during his senior year. Thanks to his history teacher, Dante was pushed into discovering things that he liked doing, which would also prepare him for college. His history teacher coached him through his first crush and was also there for him when a relationship with the crush didn't materialize.

Dante's history teacher also facilitated getting him to and from his debating tournaments which Dante appreciated as he enjoyed the interactions during these trips. For all these reasons, Dante identifies his history teacher as being the only positive male role model in his life growing up until he went off to college.

Being a Mentor

Although he does not do face-to-face mentoring, Dante provides career/professional mentorship to students he has met during his professional journey and through various organizations with which he has maintained relationships. This is mainly done via phone or through social media since his relocation to Charleston from Florida. Dante has provided mentorship through recommendations and advice to those who needed a more committed approach with their personal and professional lives.

Dante mentioned that he also provided community mentorship to black males on campus during his grad school years and has also been on the advisory board for several black male initiatives on college campuses.

JASON ELLIS

Hometown: Anderson, SC
Education Level: Ph.D. Doctorate
Occupation: Electrical Engineer/Software Developer
Married: No
Kids: No

Jason's father was around when he was a baby until around the age of six. He was in and out between households with Jason, his sister, and two half-brothers. His father was in his life to some degree, but not very much. He saw him occasionally because he was in a town about 20 minutes away, but he no longer lived in the house with Jason. When he did see him, it was not on a regular, consistent basis. His mom would take him and his sister to visit him once in a while and would say, 'Hey, spend some time with your dad.' After he turned maybe six or seven, his primary interaction with his dad was Jason calling every once in a while, just to talk.

The Cool Evolution

When Jason's dad was around, it was great. He would always tell people his dad was the definition of cool. He would say they were Stylistics, Four Tops, and The Temptations levels of cool. Most times, when he was around, things were pretty good. The problem was that his father was an alcoholic, and when he drank, he would tend to get crazy.

Jason had several fond memories of him from when he was a child. He remembers listening to music and just hanging out, going fishing, and doing stuff like that when he was around. Also, his dad got sick when Jason got older. His theater had congestive heart failure. His sister was living in Atlanta during that time. His brothers were just not as dependable, and so Jason became his de facto caretaker. He would take him to his doctors' appointments, that kind of thing. Jason got to see a much different, more vulnerable side of him during those years, which were many years of his life before he passed away. Jason came to realize how much he cared for his family. He taught him about the capacity to love. Jason believes love is something that evolves, and our ability to love other people grows. When someone says they love you and then do stupid stuff, it doesn't mean that they don't love you. It's just that they have a smaller capacity to love you unconditionally.

Jason's father was the one who helped him develop that theory, and he didn't understand that when he was young. All he knew was this guy, his father, liked to do stupid stuff all the time. But as Jason grew older, he would hear the conversations and saw a more vulnerable side of his father. He began to understand a little bit more about people's capacity to love.

Relationship Observations

His dad was an alcoholic, and he was abusive to his mom. Everything that Jason did was done to try not to be like him. Jason has never been much of a drinker. He's always had an unquestionable level of respect for women and was very protective of his mother and sister. Jason took on that 'man of the house' role at a very young age. In that regard, it probably matured Jason faster than maybe some other kids just because he had seen and heard things that kids probably shouldn't see and hear.

Regrets

His father expressed some regrets about being absent from his life. Honestly, he had more talks like when he was young, and his father would call when he was drunk. He would get candid with Jason when he was drunk. That's when he would call and have these long in-depth conversations about all the stuff that he regretted. When he got older, it was less about talking about his regrets and more about understanding his motives and getting to know who he was because Jason had never had the opportunity to do that. Interestingly his father spoke more about his childhood and his relationship with his father and brother and understanding how he grew up. Jason found out that he had an older brother that he never met because my father had him when he was 17 and signed away his parental rights. Jason never knew him. That had a pretty significant effect on Jason's father. Jason didn't even know about this until he got older and how much that affected him. Getting to know those types of things and just getting to know his father as a man made him learn more about him as he got older.

His father expressed many regrets about the way he treated Jason's mom, which he appreciated. He never saw himself as an absent father, even though he wasn't in the house with the family. He did see his children, knew them, and talked to them on occasion. To him, that was being in their lives.

Not having a consistent relationship with his father impacted him as he grew up. He did think that it impacted him differently than some other people he knew. So many people tend to rebel when their father is not in their lives. Often, they struggle to maintain a consistent level of success or find themselves in troubling situations. Jason felt that his impact was the opposite.

Impact on Jason

Jason took the opposite path to do everything he could to not be like this guy, and he still does that. He was successful in school, stayed out of trouble, and treated the women in his life well. From his perspective, his father's actions and absence had a positive impact in many ways.

Other Positive Role Models

Jason also had a stepfather who came into his life when I was 12 years old. It was not a long period where he didn't have a male figure until that point. He was a positive father figure and helped him have a pretty good balance in his life, and Jason appreciated that.

Jason's step-father was 19 years older than his mom. He had made some similar mistakes in his life, such as not keeping his family together. He was very passionate about kids and young people and wanted to be there for his family in his old age. He was an extremely loyal and family-oriented guy.

Jason said this was a total 180 from what he had previously experienced. Previously he had this guy who had virtually no loyalty whatsoever to his family. Then he had this guy who did absolutely everything he could for his family. He wasn't perfect. He had a temper, but he was never abusive like his father was. He had issues as any man would, but he was an incredible example of what a man or a father should be like.

Being a Role Model

Jason believes he has turned out to be a positive male role model. He has faults as any man does, but he's achieved a level of success in his life. He loves his family, and he's very loyal. He tries to be generous with both his time and his finances. Jason is God-fearing, and he loves God. Jason puts that love at the forefront of his life, and he follows Christian principles and values. He thinks those are all attributes that make him a good role model. Like any young single guy, Jason can be selfish and self-absorbed at times. He tries to combat those opposing sides with as much positivity as he can. He strives to be the best version of himself that he can be.

Jason is a mentor with an organization called Distinguished Gentleman's Club (DGC), which he calls a "fantastic organization." He says that his involvement in this organization is one of the best decisions he ever made. DGC was his first opportunity to spend real time with young kids who weren't family members or friends from school. Since he was the youngest in his extended family by several years, he had never had the opportunity to be a leader. His participation in this organization has allowed him to have a new perspective.

DGC was the first time he got to see what it would be like to be a father. Jason's always questioned his ability to be a good dad because he just didn't have an excellent example for periods throughout his life. He had his stepdad, but he didn't know why he didn't have any self-confidence in the idea of parenting. He was very uncertain about what kind of person he would be and what kind of father I would be.

DGC was the first opportunity where he got to play almost that fatherly type role. It's not the same thing, but he is a role model by example and a father figure for a young developing mind, which was attractive to him. Jason was surprised when he began seeing some of those qualities within himself because he didn't know he had many of them. He didn't know that he could understand the right thing to say when a young person asks you the tough questions. To influence young people positively and see positive change happen in a young person based on your influence is a dope thing to see and experience.

The first time that he had that kind of impact, Jason was amazed. A friend of his said that it could take years to impact a young person. DGC has allowed him to have the ability to put in the time to see this impact. It's been eye-opening and astonishing and has been a surprise to him. One decision that he makes could potentially change his whole life and the life of a young person. All of this makes him wonder how much better of a dad he will be because of this group. It hasn't even just been working with kids; it's been watching the other men and fathers mentoring in the program. He sees them and wants to do what they are doing. Jason doesn't get to talk to most of his friends that are fathers now because they have families of their own. They're not hanging out anymore, so getting this different perspective and spending time interacting with guys who are fathers and interacting with them around their children has been eye-opening in many ways.

Reflections on His Father

Jason's father has passed away, and he reflects on what he would say if he had the opportunity to speak to him one last time. He stole this line from the movie "Love and Basketball." But I would probably ask him why he could never be the man he always wanted me to be?" He said this because he saw that as his dad got older, he showed a much more vulnerable side and learned that he had high hopes for his children. Even though he knew that he wasn't heavily involved in his children's lives and wasn't always the best influence, he still had high aspirations for Jason and his siblings and was proud of his kids. He talked about them a lot.

Every time Jason met one of his father's friends, they knew who he was. They knew what he had done and everything he had accomplished. He was proud and had high hopes for all of his kids. Jason would just like to ask him, 'What was it that kept you from being the guy that you knew was the right guy? What was it that kept you from being that?'

Parting Thoughts

Jason knows everybody wants the next generation to be better than theirs. He's not even a father yet, but he already wants his future kids to be better than he is. Jason feels everybody wants that. But what's stopping anyone from being that version of you? What is stopping you from doing everything that you want your kids to do? Did you just get to a point where you just give up and just resign to the fact that "this is the way that I am, and I'm never going to be different"? If you want your kids to be financially stable and financially free or live a wealthy lifestyle, what's stopping you from changing your financial habits now? If you want your kids to love their spouse, what's stopping you from doing the same thing? What is stopping you?

JEROME COLDEN

Hometown: Buffalo, NY but raised in North Augusta, SC
Education Level: Associates Degree
Occupation: Project Engineer
Married: Yes (Almost 2 years), 1 Divorce (16 years)
Kids: 2 boys (34 and 26)

Jerome's father was present in life until he was ten years old. They had a fairly decent relationship; however, his father was an alcoholic who would physically and verbally abuse his mom. When the abuse got too bad, his mom left, and they moved to South Carolina. That was the last time he saw his father. His father was never abusive towards him, though.

When Jerome and his mother moved to the south to live with his grandparents, his grandfather did not allow any visits or communication with his father. He also did not see much effort from his father, so there was no communication at all.

The relationship Jerome had with his father was okay. He always looked up to and respected him because he was his father, but he could still tell that something about him was not quite right.

Catching Up

At the age of 21, Jerome was going on a trip to Europe and was passing through Buffalo, NY, where his father was residing. He found out that his father had cancer, so he stopped in to visit him while he was in the hospital. Being on his deathbed, Jerome wanted to let his father know that he did not harbor any ill will or negative feelings towards him. He told him that he respected his decisions as he was only a child but that he would never make the same mistakes he did, and that was a lesson that he learned from him.

He left after saying his condolences if something would happen to him during his trip to Europe that was the last he saw of his father.

Other Role Models

Jerome never missed the communication with his father as his grandfather immediately stepped in to fill the father role in his life. He found it to be a breath of fresh air as he learned so much from his grandfather during the 17 years he spent with him. He felt that he learned more from his grandfather than he had learned from his father in the first ten years of his life. Jerome also speaks highly of his much older brother, who would take on a role as a father figure. His brother was still living in New York, but he would keep Jerome on the straight and narrow whenever he strayed in the absence of his grandparents through phone conversations. Jerome now shares a similar relationship with his grandson. He believes he doesn't have to be physically present to positively impact as long as a level of respect has been established.

Jerome's grandfather was an entrepreneur who owned his own business. He instilled in him the importance of a good work ethic and how to save money. Jerome would work for his grandfather during the summer months, where he would be paid and made to save his money. This money was used to do his back-to-school shopping instead of getting what his grandmother wanted to buy. His grandfather was also the lead deacon at his church and taught Jerome many lessons from that aspect of his life. There was a lot he learned from his grandfather over the 17 years he spent with him.

Hard Work

Jerome remembers getting his school bus driver's license when he was in the 10th grade. In South Carolina, one was allowed to apply for this license at the age of 16. Transporting other students to and back from school was a huge responsibility. Jerome would wake up at 5 am each morning to start his route at 6 am. Once finished for the day, he would park the bus at home. He remembers his grandfather being proud of having the school bus parked in their yard and how he would beat him home so he could see him park the school bus, all with a big grin on his face.

Jerome would like to let his grandfather know how grateful he is for the lessons he taught him as a youth. There was a lot he didn't understand about why his grandfather did the things that he did. He thought many of these things were crazy and would often wonder why his grandfather had him doing them. One such activity was having him in the field every weekend planting or harvesting crops or slaughtering their animal to make meat for their smokehouse. He now looks back and realizes that the only thing the family had to go to the grocery store for was paper products. If they needed meat, they would go to their smokehouse and get it, and if they required fruits or vegetables, they would visit the refrigerator.

He remembers looking at it then as being work. He is now grateful that his grandfather taught him those lessons, as he can do the same for himself now if he needs to. For this, he would want to thank him.

Jerome learned what not to do when it comes to his role as a family member from his father. From his grandfather, he understood what to do as it pertained to cultivating and growing his family.

Passing It On

Jerome said he would teach his sons respect for their fellow men and the importance of a good work ethic. These were the two most essential traits that his grandfather would instill in him. He shared a saying from his grandfather, who would always say, "You could best believe as you get older, you're going to find out that because of who you are, you're going to have to work double hard or twice as hard to level the playing field." Jerome didn't always understand what he was saying then, but its meaning became crystal clear as he got older.

Jerome believes he is a positive role model as he tries to instill many of the lessons he learned growing up on the folks that cross his path today. He shares his special love for teenage boys as he remembers how difficult it was to transition from boyhood to manhood. He tries at every opportunity to help them along as long as they are willing, wanting, or seeking that help. He says, "it is easier to help those that want the help."

Being a Role Model

Jerome enjoys mentoring and has been involved with The Distinguished Gentleman's Club for almost two years. Jerome says he assesses the child's needs and does his best to expose them to as many opportunities as possible to see the world as they would never otherwise experience.

One such activity he did was take his mentees to see the historic sites in the downtown Charleston area. He got the idea after he did a similar activity for his son's school project. His son was tasked with visiting these same historical sites and getting a photo and an information card. They then had to write something about each area they had seen. He thought it was a clever way to expose the children to these places and get the parents involved because they would need to take the kids around. He found this exposure to be a great educational tool.

Jerome feels that knowing that you have impacted these kids' lives, no matter how minute it might seem to us, is much more significant to them. As they grow older, they will learn to appreciate it more. This is the gratitude Jerome gets from mentorship.

"CHRISTOPHER ROBINSON"

Hometown: North Charleston, SC
Education Level: Pursuing Associates Degree
Occupation: Administrative Assistant
Married: No
Children: No

Christopher's father was in his life growing up but did not play an active role. His parents divorced when he was 12 years old. He says his father was "out and about" in the world due to drug addiction and its associated issues. The earliest that he can remember that something was wrong was when he was in the 4th grade.

When his parents split up, he viewed it as a good thing because his parents didn't have a good relationship. He was happy that his mother could be free of the issues that came with the drug addiction.

Christopher doesn't remember having much of a father-son bond with his father. They didn't do much together, which led to him teaching himself many things that a father would generally teach his son. He also didn't fear his father growing up, but he did have respect for him.

He recalls getting in trouble as a child for doing things to help his father when he came back from one of his drug-fueled absences. He recalls letting his father in the house, giving him food, etc., which led to Christopher being scolded by the other family members.

He doesn't harbor any resentment towards his father because Christopher believes that everything happens for a reason, and it's how one deals with it that matters in the end.

Once Christopher's father got clean, he got back into the church and started doing the right thing, making it easier to be around him. Now they have a "friendship," and they speak often. His father views him as his best friend.

If he could say anything to his father, he would say, "I'm proud of the man that I've become, and I don't blame you for your path in life because it is what it is."

Other Role Models

Christopher didn't have anyone step up in his father's absence to serve as a role model or mentor. He thinks that things probably would've been better for him growing up if he would've had a male role model. He does believe that he turned out okay without one, though. Christopher had older uncles that he didn't know and were not present in his life. The one uncle that he did know/have a relationship with was the same age as he was, so this did not make him a good candidate as "role model" material.

When he was 12 or 13 years old, a gentleman came into his life who was interested in his musical ability and helped cultivate it. That's the closest thing that comes to mind for him in terms of mentorship. As he got older, around 20 years old, he met a minister who positively influenced and saved his life. He says that the minister was there for him in a dark time.

Being a Role Model

Christopher does not mentor formally, but he does have nephews that he encourages to do the right things in school and their homes. Christopher believes that he is a positive male role model because he's true to himself and has good energy. He believes that you reap what you sow, and he tries to sow good deeds and make people smile.

MCKENDRICK DUNN

Hometown: Augusta, GA
Education Level: Bachelor's Degree in Mathematics
Occupation: Materials Leader
Married: Yes (14 years)
Kids: 2 (1 boy 18, 1 girl 15)

McKendrick's father was in his life as he grew up. His parents got married when he was five years old and divorced when he was in college. There was a time where his father was physically abusive to his mother. McKendrick has a hard time recalling many fond memories of his father. He does remember waking up to the sounds of his father abusing his mother. Most of his positive memories as a child were centered around his mom.

According to McKendrick, his relationship with his father was "okay" in the beginning. There was a separation because his father traveled a lot because of his job in the military. Shortly after he was born, his father joined the army, which led to McKendrick spending most of his childhood with his mother and grandmother. The result of this distance was a disconnect between his father and himself.

There was a lack of stability at home, and he felt that he had no one to go to for talks. As McKendrick got older, his father began having more discussions regarding becoming a mature man, speaking to women, being respectful, etc. His father wasn't the type to show a lot of emotion around his family and rarely showed feelings about anything.

Life Lessons

McKendrick's family did not have much money growing up, so most of the time that he recalls spending with his dad was centered around learning to do things that would save them money. When he got older, his father was adamant about him learning about cars. It was common for him to wake up early in the morning to take all of the shoestrings out of his shoes and clean them with a toothbrush because he never knew when he'd get another pair. Though he values the lessons he learned from his father, he doesn't look back on his childhood interactions with his father with any particular fondness.

At the time of this interview, McKendrick's father was still alive and still lived in the same area. He had also gotten remarried. Their relationship has significantly improved since McKendrick became an adult. After his parents' divorce, they continued to live in the same city and even attended the same church as they did when they were married. His dad still had the same mentality he's always had regarding insecurities about his financial future, Overall they have a better relationship. McKendrick spoke to his father once a week and visited him whenever he went back to visit his hometown. He remarked that his brothers did not share this renewed relationship with their father.

Words for His Father

If he could say anything to his father, McKendrick would begin by stating his disappointment with his father's lack of commitment to his mother. He believes that the distance between him and his father was primarily due to his father's failure to commit to his mother. This led to resentment on his part. He is thankful that he has mended the relationship at this point, but McKendrick lost a great deal of time. He would also tell him that he's grateful for having a father because he recognizes that not everyone has a father that they could call on.

Becoming a Father

The stoic nature of his father impacted the way McKendrick parented his children as they were growing up. He has never been one to show a lot of emotion, and he credits his wife for being intentional with giving his children the emotional support they need. He feels that structure and stability are things that he valued, and he doesn't feel as though he has invested much in changing that within himself. McKendrick finds that as a father, he realized that you can't always be rigid with children and that flexibility is necessary. His wife has helped him in this regard.

McKendrick says that his relationship with his son is good. He feels that he's been intentional in raising his son by instilling lifelong principles into his son. He allows his son to find his way in many instances, but he also makes an effort to teach his son about specific principles he deems essential. One such focus is teaching him to give his maximum effort in anything that he does. As his son has gotten older, he has made efforts to create opportunities for him and his son to have conversations via what they call "Talk Tuesday." This is the time that he set aside expressly to have conversations with his son. At first, his son didn't say much, but he began to open up as time went on. These discussions were no-holds-barred conversations that allowed them to build an open dialogue of communication.

Being a Husband

McKendrick's experiences with his father also shaped him as a husband. His father wasn't faithful to his mother. He believes this, in addition to financial issues, led to his parent's divorce. He has always been determined not to duplicate the behaviors/activities/deficiencies that led to his parent's divorce with that knowledge. Religion was another critical piece that caused a chasm in his parents' marriage. In his words, his mother matured spiritually ahead of his father. When they got divorced, his father found his way into the church. This occurred when it was too late for the marriage to be saved.

Being a Role Model

McKendrick believes himself to be a good role model because of his willingness to intentionally create ways for his children to have a bright future. Due to the success that both he and his wife have achieved, he realizes that is a tall task. He feels sure that they are more than capable of achieving their goals. He tries his best to be good to his family, friends, and anybody he interacts with.

McKendrick is conscious of his drive to be respectful of people's time and space. He shares an anecdote about people coming to stay at his home. He has timers set on all of the televisions in the house to go off at 12:30 am. Initially, he wanted his children to sleep without hearing a tv all night long when they had visitors. He has always wanted positive energy around his children and thus walks the walk he has set for them.

He also serves his community as a mentor. For three years, McKendrick volunteered by teaching economics classes with the Junior Achievement program. After he graduated college, he moved back to his hometown and became a mentor at his church through the World Ambassadors' program. This continued until he moved for career purposes. Before proceeding, he was offered the position of director of the organization at his church, but he turned down the role since he knew he would be moving. The organization set up outings and events for the youth around the church. After moving to the Charleston area, he once again dove into youth initiatives within the church. This time, he was working with the children's church which he did for two years. During that time, his son joined the Distinguished Gentlemen's Club Mentor Organization at his middle school. The founder, Ricardo Perry, reached out to him about joining as a mentor, and he agreed.

McKendrick stepped away from the children's church when his wife got a promotion that pulled her out of the home for frequent travel because it limited his time availability. He has maintained his relationship with the church despite not teaching children's church anymore. Since graduating high school, his son has continued advocating to mentor with the Distinguished Gentlemen's Club and serve as the organization's Program Director.

McKendrick loves seeing the young men learn, grow and experience new things. Giving "small pieces" of himself to these young men fills his heart with joy. He enjoys providing stability to young men who otherwise may not have it. He remembers moving to ten different schools while growing up and lacking stability. He takes great pride in providing that stability for young men. He feels that it is a must to give back to the community he lives and works in.

PARTING THOUGHTS

From the start of writing this book on November 30, 2017, to today, June 22, 2021, three years, six months, and twenty-three days have passed. In that time frame, so much has changed. My father passed away, I've left the classroom to become a leader in the not-for-profit sector, and I've become the Executive Director of Lowcountry Youth Services (even the name of our organization has changed.) I've also completed this labor of love by being able to meet some great people and learn from their incredible stories. They spanned in age, race, religion, and socioeconomic status. Still, the one constant was that, as I expected, each of them had a fantastic story that I was honored to be able to document. Some people were comfortable sharing their names, and some went with aliases. I minded neither because I understand some of the pain drawn upon just to remember these stories. I can remember being emotional while conducting several of these interviews. A few had to take a break just to compose themselves. Despite that, no one stopped me from documenting their stories. This is an era where embracing mental health and advocating for men to express their emotions is crucial. I was happy to have been a part of letting them share these emotions. For some of these men, this was a form of therapy. For me, it was the same.

I mentioned that my father passed away. When my father passed away, I didn't know how to process the loss and move forward. He was the final person that I interviewed for this book. We knew that he was short on time due to a bout with cancer, and we thought we'd have more time together.

On July 10, 2018, I interviewed my father to document HIS story as a part of my book. I wanted to finish the book before he passed away so he could read it. We didn't have that long. My father passed away on August 14, a month after our interview. With that in mind, this book is dedicated to my father, Herbert Lee Jenkins Jr. I know that he is proud to see what I've accomplished, and I also know that this book will ensure that his name lives on. I love you always, #getdownPop!

For those who have read this book, I hope it inspires you to tell your story, and I hope that you found some answers of your own in the pages of this book. I asked the question, "Is it important for boys to have positive male role models?" I believe in the stories of these men; we've found that it is. When those relationships are missing, there's a gap that someone must fill. I hope this book allows you to look at your own life and ask yourself, "Am I filling the gap?" "Can I do more?" "Am I the type of father/husband/example that my child would speak well of when I'm no longer here?" I know… more questions.

BUT the great thing is, as I said at the beginning of the book, "All knowledge begins with a question."

Illustration: Cedric Tolliver II

CPSIA information can be obtained
at www.ICGtesting.com
Printed in the USA
BVHW021407130821
614281BV00022B/1233